Nicholas James has a degree in law and politics, which he hated, though he did notice that the lawyer with the best story usually won the case. Having met his wife while they were both working in marketing, he quit his job with the aim of becoming a writer, doing a crash course in plumbing to earn some money on the side. But the plumbing soon became a thriving, full-time business, so writing had to take a back seat. On the plus side, he always had funny, nail-biting plumbing stories to tell. Over twenty years of working as a plumber, Nick has amassed a wealth of material; the pandemic lockdown finally gave him a chance to write his stories down, and *Pipe Dreams* is the result.

PIPE DREAMS

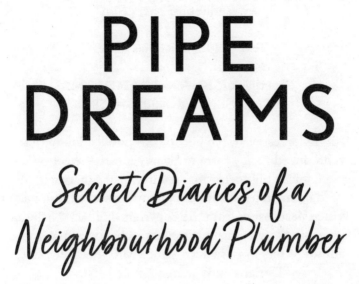

Secret Diaries of a Neighbourhood Plumber

NICHOLAS JAMES

△L
AD LIB

First published in 2023 by Ad Lib Publishers Ltd
15 Church Road
London SW13 9HE
www.adlibpublishers.com

Paperback ISBN 978-1-802470-93-2
eBook ISBN 978-1-802470-58-1

A CIP catalogue record for this book is available from the British Library.

Printed in the UK
10 9 8 7 6 5 4 3 2 1

I'd like to dedicate this book to five people: my parents, Janet and Tony, whose ability to laugh at life inspired me to tell funny stories; and my wonderful wife and children, whose belief, patience, love and support spurred me on to write it.

Contents

1

Baptism of Fire

I cut the pipe. Once I'd done that, there was no way back. I was working in a top-floor flat in Farringdon in central London. I'd frozen the pipe to fit a new stopcock, because I needed to move it and I couldn't gain access to the main stop valve. I realised almost immediately that I'd made a mistake about the width of the pipe and now I had no way of stopping the water when the ice plug melted. This meant I had just twenty minutes to find another fitting, otherwise I was going to flood the whole building.

I started to panic. My pupils dilated and I felt really light-headed. I thought I was going to have a heart attack. Normally, I would jump into my van and get another fitting, but I didn't have my van with me as there had been nowhere to park. The only solution was to run as fast as I could to the nearest plumbing merchant, which was at least ten minutes away. When I got there I was covered in sweat. I could hardly talk I was panting so hard. There was a long queue inside, but I barged past everyone, apologising profusely, explaining that it was an emergency. Fortunately, the guy behind the counter took pity on me and gave me what I needed. I turned round and ran as fast as I could back to the flat. When I got there the pipe was just starting to thaw. There was the tiniest droplet of water dangling from the end of it. If I had been a minute longer I would have been too late. I would have flooded the place and my life as a plumber would have been over before it had even properly begun. I quickly pushed the fitting onto the pipe and tightened it up. Then, I collapsed on the floor.

At that precise moment, my client walked in with several middle-aged men who looked as if they might be of Mayan descent. They were carrying a variety of musical instruments, mostly of a kind I had never seen before. They said they were a *bolero* and *son* band. I immediately thought of the TV series *Steptoe and Son* and the image of a Caribbean rag-and-bone band popped into my mind. I overheard them say that they were on their way to Glastonbury. They obviously didn't realise I could speak Spanish, because they also remarked that they thought I'd been sleeping on the job. Little did they know ... As they disappeared into the front room, the ice plug I'd created earlier gave way, and I heard the surge of water push against the back of the fitting. I held my breath and prayed as the song '*Chan Chan*' wafted gently out of the windows and flowed down the road towards the stalls at the end of Exmouth Market. The new fitting held and there weren't any leaks.

I hadn't heard '*Chan Chan*' since I'd been travelling in Central America in the early nineties. Revolution was in the air back then. The Zapatistas had shot up a bus full of tourists on their way to San Cristóbal de las Casas in Mexico. I was supposed to have been on that bus; I'd missed it by only a couple of minutes. At the time, I'd been weaving my way from country to country, sleeping in hammocks, visiting ancient Mayan monuments and trying to work out what I wanted to do with my life. I had last heard that song in San Pedro, on the shores of Lake Atitlan in Guatemala, where I was supposed to be meeting some friends. I could see their faces, as clearly as when we said goodbye behind the time-worn temples of Tulum, our hair matted from endless exposure to salt and sand.

Back in the flat, I sat up and considered the sink I was working on, reclaimed from the Old London Hospital, where Joseph Merrick, 'the so-called 'Elephant Man', had been treated. It looked like it was from that period and it had taps with long arms, of the sort that surgeons can turn on and off with their elbows. It seemed a strange choice, but that did rather sum up the guy I was working for. He was decidedly strange. It was as if he was travelling in a different dimension, full of beats and rhythms from faraway lands. Practical things just seemed to pass him by. He was a struggling artist; and he probably always would be. He wasn't the kind of musician who was suddenly going to get a record deal and become a multimillionaire. He was going to be tapping his bongos in that slightly run-down council flat for the rest of his life, and there was nothing wrong with that; I respected him for it. He didn't want material things, he was striving for something better than that. He was looking for inner satisfaction, and drumming helped him to find it.

As the music continued, more and more images from my travels kept flashing into my mind. Swimming in the clear, fresh pools of Agua Azul in Mexico; sleeping below the pyramids of Palenque, surrounded by howler monkeys and jaguars; and walking down the deserted white sand beaches of Tulum as the sun set behind the ruins. I'd travelled with my friends for almost a month, but I had to go back to Mexico City to spend Christmas with my family, so I agreed to meet them in a bar in San Pedro on the 3rd of January. In the end, I was two days late because of the unrest – the Mexican government had closed the border with Guatemala. There were no mobile phones back then so I had no way of letting them know I'd been held up. By the time I got there, they'd already left.

As I lay on that dusty bathroom floor, it occurred to me that my new life was freeing my mind to drift in a way that it hadn't done in years, as those catchy Caribbean riffs took me back to that candle-lit bar on the edge of Lake Atitlán all those years ago.

My life wasn't supposed to be like this. I wasn't meant to be changing stopcocks in council flats. I could conjugate Latin verbs, I had a law degree, my parents had spent a small fortune on my education, yet here I was, lying on the floor with a wrench in my hand. As my heart palpitations began to subside, I sat up and started slowly to dismantle the bath, while those bongo beats bounced off the walls, soothing my senses and filling the building with a renewed hope of summer.

By the time I finally decided to call it a day, the sun was just starting to dip down behind the old Finsbury town hall. I felt like I'd been in a different world all day. That was the first big job I did as a plumber. Up to that point, I'd always worked in an office. I'd been a senior account handler in one of the top marketing agencies in London and was being groomed for the top job. I had all the right qualifications and experience, but everything changed when my son was born. I suddenly felt as if I was leading someone else's life. So, after many long discussions with my very understanding wife, Jo, I decided to give it all up to pursue my dream of becoming a writer, on the understanding that I would also train to become a plumber to help pay the bills. Jo was incredibly supportive at a time when a lot of partners wouldn't have been. She encouraged me and reassured me that everything would be okay, in the way that only a truly wonderful wife would.

Jo and I had met at a small marketing agency in a building overlooking Hertford Castle. It was strangely romantic. During the summer we'd have lunch sitting on the grass, watching the water cascade over the weir. It was obvious from the moment we met that we were perfect for each other. Ours was a real love affair. There were no white sand beaches or ancient Mayan ruins, at least not at the start. We fell in love over Excel spreadsheets and press passes at printers in Potters Bar and Peterborough, but we were made for each other. The combination of our characters and the chemistry between us meant that our life together was always dramatic. Now we were going to start the second act.

Most of my friends thought I was having a premature mid-life crisis when I told them I was going to become a plumber, while I pursued my ambitions as a writer. My parents thought I'd gone completely mad. I was, after all, entirely rejecting the life that they'd envisioned for me. I didn't see it that way. I looked at it in a far more practical way. I wanted to be involved in bringing up my kids, and I didn't want to be stuck in an office any more. I was sick of working for other people and I wanted to write a book.

There was a shortage of plumbers at the time, and I figured I'd never be out of work. I never was.

I've worked as a plumber for a complete cross-section of society: judges and drug addicts; rock stars and railway workers; Oscar winners and obstetricians. I've employed astrophysicists and alcoholics. Some of the tradesmen I've worked with may have been terrorists; my carpenter *was* an ex-convict; my plasterer was also a prop maker for feature films; and my electrician used to be a theatrical agent. I'm told that I challenge social norms and that I cross the social divide. I'm not sure if that's true, but I'm certainly interested in people and I really don't care where they come from or what they do for a living.

I've often wondered what would have happened if I hadn't made it back in time to prevent a flood in that council flat in Clerkenwell. Once an ice plug melts, you can't refreeze it – you can't freeze moving water. There would have been no way to stop it flooding the entire building. My client had no idea what I had just gone through when he walked in with that balding bolero band and saw me lying on the floor. At the end of the day, I closed the door behind me and made my way down the open concrete staircase to the street below. They were still playing their hypnotic Latin love songs and people were starting to gather in the street outside. I'm sure most of them didn't understand a word of Spanish, but that didn't matter. They were being transported to that distant land, where pirates once prevailed, where the hot, humid air is thick with cigar smoke and the rum runs freely on every street corner. As I crossed the road, crowds were gathering at the end of Exmouth Market, eating falafel and drinking bottled beers.

It occurred to me that however stressful my day had been, it had also been stimulating and exhilarating. It was a world away from the monotony of office life that I had so recently left behind. I felt like I'd just got off a commuter train, where I'd been wedged into someone's armpit for the last ten years, and I was now finally free. I knew then that I was doing the right thing. Just like I did when I went travelling around Central America. My life hadn't turned out as I'd hoped it would and I knew I had to do something about it. I was never going to be your average plumber, but that could be to my advantage. As I walked down the centre of that pedestrian parade with those bolero beats gradually fading away into the background, I was hoping that my new life would introduce me to a colourful cast of characters and would furnish me with a unique stock of stories that would inspire me to write a book. It just took me another twenty years to actually write it.

2

Merry Band of Misfits

Over the years, my life has taken me in some very unexpected directions. If someone had told me when I was eighteen that I would become a plumber and that my son would be a ballet dancer, I would have laughed at them. It's ironic really, since it was the birth of my son, Oliver, that propelled my life in such a different direction, yet his has always seemed to be set in stone. Some people are just born for the theatre; it's in their genes. Oli is one of them. He was always extremely flexible. As a baby, his legs went over his head – no problem. 'Watch this, Woo,' we used to say to him, lifting his legs over his head. He loved it, laughing every time we did it. We showed everyone; it was our baby party trick.

When he was born, Jo started working for her father, a songwriter. When Oli was eighteen months old, Jo's dad showcased a musical he'd written to try to attract potential producers. Oli went to all the rehearsals and every performance. He just loved it. He sat in the female dressing room for hours and all the women cooed over him. In retrospect, that may have been where he developed his interest in tights! As a toddler, he never stopped moving and no matter what we did, nothing ever tired him out. Before we had him, Jo worked for Universal Pictures and looked after their musical releases on video (that's how long ago it was). As a result, we had a lot of them knocking around the flat. *Joseph and His Amazing Technicolour Dreamcoat* was Oli's first favourite. He was totally mesmerised by it. 'Jophus, Jophus! I want to watch Jophus,' he would shout as soon as he saw a television. He sat in front of that video for hours. Then, after he'd seen it twenty times, he stood up, turned his back to the TV, and performed it. He sang, acted and danced the whole show. He played every part. He didn't know what any of the words actually meant and could barely say most of them, but that didn't stop him; he was away. It was hilarious; he'd clearly found his passion.

Now, all we had to do was feed it. So, from that moment on, all our spare money went on theatre tickets. Jo found a dance school and off he went. Ballet, tap, street dance … you name it, he did it. 'Jophus', *Cats*, *Singin' in the Rain*, *The Sound of Music* … he knew them all. He played every part, sang every song; by the time he was six, he knew the entire script of every musical. Then, his ballet teacher came to us and said, 'I really think he's got something. I'd like to teach him one on one.' And that was it. Three years later, she put him forward for the Junior Associates at The Royal Ballet School and, much to our amazement, he got in. It wasn't long before his theatrical life advanced even further, and he was still only eleven. The Junior Associates led on to The Royal Ballet School. Ninette de Valois's Sadler's Wells Ballet School was granted the use of the White Lodge in the centre of Richmond Park in 1955. The following year, the school was granted a Royal Charter and became The Royal Ballet School. It is an absolutely amazing place, originally built as a hunting lodge for King George I and has had royal connections ever since. In the Grand Salon hang pictures of the royal family dating back to Queen Victoria. When Oli was offered a place, we were both elated and also slightly shocked. It hadn't ever been our intention to send him away to boarding school. In fact, I had vowed that I would never inflict that on him. But The Royal Ballet School was different. We weren't sending him there to get rid of him, as my parents had done to me; Oli was begging us to be allowed to go. He was being offered a place because of his talent, not because of our bank balance. He wanted to go there more than anything else in the world and we didn't feel it was our place to stop him. It felt like we were in our very own version of *Billy Elliot*, and I was determined I was not going to be like Billy's dad.

Jo was absolutely devastated. She cried every time we dropped him off, so much so that I used to joke that I'd installed a cryometer in the car! Jo comes from a large Jewish family. She understands herself better than anyone else I know – as she should, having had years of therapy – but that didn't stop her mourning the loss of Oli for the next seven years.

I also cried when Oli got into The Royal Ballet School, but for a very different reason. What the film *Billy Elliot* doesn't tell you is that The Royal Ballet School isn't free for everyone: it's means tested, to ensure that no child is excluded as a result of their parent's financial standing. I like that, as it squares with my politics. The problem for us, though, was the way in which they assessed parental wealth. It was a bit like having to pay tax twice, except The Royal Ballet School didn't take any of our expenditure into account; they looked only at our income. So, suddenly we had to find a way to pay for Oli's education. Normal plumbing jobs just didn't cut it any more; I had to branch out and take on bigger jobs, ones which I could project manage as well as doing all the plumbing work myself. That was how I came to meet Judith.

★ ★ ★ ★

Judith was an actress. She may have been small in stature, but what she lacked in height, she certainly made up for in personality. She had lived for the past twenty years in Bloomsbury and had worked, pretty much without a break, from the moment she left drama school (which is quite an achievement for an actress). Then, as she approached middle age, the parts had started to dry up, so she moved out of central London and went mortgage-free. She sold her flat in Bloomsbury and bought a two-bedroom flat in Friern Barnet, which needed a lot of work. That was where I came in. What she wanted was really quite quirky, which pretty accurately reflected who she was. I liked her instantly. She was very quick-witted and extremely funny. Her boyfriend was also a client of mine. He, too, was extremely funny and quite eccentric. He used to write lying down, literally lying on the floor with an improvised desk suspended above him. After I finished building his bathroom, he put a life-sized female mannequin at the end of the shower with a towel carefully draped over its arm. Then he put two more at either end of the bath. It amused him.

'It certainly is an original look,' said Judith, as she inspected my work when she popped over for tea. Thinking back on it, I don't believe I ever actually gave her a price to renovate her flat. She simply told me what she wanted, and I told her how I was going to do it. She trusted me, and I trusted her. She was ambitious and she knew what she wanted. So, I set about putting a team together. She called them my 'Merry Band of Misfits', and she was right: that was exactly what we were. Misfits we might have been, but we were all very good at what we did. When you work closely with people in tough situations, you tend to ignore their faults and just like them for who they are. I came to regard The Misfits as my friends and I knew I could rely on them when the chips were down.

We were essentially a very loose coalition of tradespeople who regularly came together to renovate people's flats. We shared work between us in a collaborative way. There was Ryan, my accidental assistant. I acquired him while I was building a bathroom in Belsize Park and somehow he sporadically kept working for me for the next ten years. Ryan was a burly Irishman with a huge scar down the right side of his face. He was a complicated concoction of contradictions, but he was also one of the bravest men I'd ever met. On the first day we worked together, he caught someone trying to steal my tools out of the back of my van. Ryan grabbed him and told him that if he ever did that again, he'd kill him, and he meant it. Violence was never far away with Ryan. It seemed to constantly simmer under the surface, but there were no-go zones with Ryan and his past was definitely one of them. He didn't have a passport or a bank account and no one seemed to know his last name. I paid him at the end of each week. He paid his rent and then drank the rest. But he was a very good plumber and he'd turn his hand to absolutely anything, even if he did start to run out of steam at around two o'clock in the afternoon as his alcohol levels started to drop.

Then there was Chris, the carpenter. Chris had been caught with a quantity of weed when he was a teenager; as a result, he'd served eighteen months in Pentonville. Chris was as honest as the day was long, he didn't do drugs, he hardly drank, but he did overcompensate for those criminal capers that had put him behind bars by taking communication with clients to the next level. He explained everything he was going to do before he did it. He'd tell you not only the size of the screws he was going to use, but also all the other sizes that were available. Then, just when you were ready to cut your own ears off, he would explain why he had decided on that particular size and its benefits over all the other sizes.

You either loved him or loathed him. I loved him, and so did Judith, but he drove everyone else crazy. Ryan wore ear protectors every day just to block him out, but Judith and I both found him amusing. We'd ask him lots of leading questions then walk away smiling just as he was getting going. I know that might sound cruel, but Chris knew he was a bit of a bore. He couldn't help it. There was a glint in his eye as he started his soliloquies. It was as if he wanted someone to cut him short. Judith and I became the Imodium that helped him overcome his verbal diarrhoea.

But for all his flaws, he was without doubt the most honest, hard-working, trustworthy tradesman I'd ever met. He always went the extra mile and most of his clients absolutely adored him. He may have been a true-blue Tory (and thought Mrs Thatcher was the bee's knees), which was a bit weird since he lived in a subsidised council flat and paid hardly any rent, but his politics was his business. The bottom line was: he was a bloody good carpenter and wouldn't put up a shelf unless he could hang from it. Ryan used to joke that he wouldn't put up a shelf unless he could hang Chris from it! Such was the comedy amongst comrades.

Another 'misfit' was Big Pete. He was six foot seven and weighed almost twenty stone. He didn't often need a ladder to plaster a ceiling. He had huge hands and an enormous cannon tattooed across his chest – he was a mad Arsenal fan. He too suffered from verbal diarrhoea, in his case drug-induced. Big Pete had a nose like a hoover: speed, coke, Mycil foot powder ... you name it, Pete shoved it up his hooter. He drank ten pints every day, but I never saw him obviously pissed. He was a complete animal. His whole metabolism had gone. He looked utterly terrifying, but when you got to know him, he was actually a real gentle giant. A true gentleman, if not in the normal sense of the word. He told me some fairly eye-watering stories about an ex-girlfriend who rather liked root vegetables. Nevertheless, he was always a gentleman to me and I always enjoyed his company immensely.

Big Pete was without doubt the most well-read plasterer in London. This was partly because he suffered from terrible insomnia, probably because of all the drugs he had in his system. Whenever Big Pete was on site, we always had the most fascinating deep philosophical discussions. He was a confirmed communist and yet he was also a raging royalist. He talked about the Queen as if she was his own mum. He also sang Neil Diamond like his life depended on it and he was always extremely entertaining. He may have had his problems, but don't we all. He was fundamentally a decent human being, an original thinker and a philosopher: a real lovable rogue and completely unique. The kind of man that can be made only in London and I loved him for it.

Then there was Dale. I don't know his real name. We called him Dale because he came from the Yorkshire Dales. He was five foot five and he too weighed over twenty stone; he also had no teeth. His centre of gravity was just below his knees. He was well over sixty, had started smoking when he was ten and had spent the past fifty years with a fag hanging out of the side of his mouth. As a result, he was always red-faced and sounded like a steam train. When he spoke, it was like listening to Darth Vader on holiday in Darlington. Dale was a heart attack waiting to happen. Whenever he got into my van it tipped markedly to one side. He ate two full English breakfasts every morning before he came to work. I spent most of the time worrying he was going to drop down dead, which he did, but we'll get to that.

For me, Dale personified everything that was great about the north of England. He said it exactly how he saw it. Oscar Wilde once said that anyone who calls a spade a spade should be forced to use one. Well, Dale did and he didn't see anything demeaning in doing so. He was proud of what he did for a living and he was bloody good at it. He was without doubt the best brickie I ever met and one of the best blokes. He insisted we listened to the cricket whenever Yorkshire were playing and then referred to the other side as shandy-drinking southerners, even if they were playing Lancashire. Everyone respected Dale. He had the kind of gravitas you get only from spending fifty years on a building site. One day when Big Pete was banging on about the sophisticated nature of Jean-Paul Sartes's existentialism, Dale Interrupted and said, 'Don't talk to me about sophistication, I've been to Leeds!'

I later found out he was quoting Vic Reeves, but his timing was impeccable and it had us all in stitches for weeks.

Our electrician was Fiona, Fi for short. She was a butch, dungaree-and-Doc-Marten-wearing tradeswoman. She looked like an East German shot putter. Everyone was scared of Fi; I was terrified of her. She had been a theatrical agent, but unfortunately she wasn't sufficiently judicious in her choice of clientele and had been forced to close. Fi was without doubt the most misogynistic person I've ever met. At first, I thought it was just an act: her attempt at trying to fall in with building-site banter, but I quickly learned that it wasn't. Fi really didn't like women, even though she was one … although I did occasionally wonder. But Fi was rock-solid reliable, and I liked her total honesty and enjoyed her company no end, even though I did sometimes find her slightly scary.

Judith was going to be living in her new flat the whole time the job was progressing, so we needed to keep it clean and habitable at the same time as we systematically smashed it apart. We also needed to limit those working to just two or three tradespeople a day, or we would be on top of each other. I co-ordinated everything, as well as doing the plumbing. This meant I let everyone know when they would be needed, otherwise they would all go off and do other jobs, which they did, but again, I'll get to that. My management style was to kill everyone with kindness and then hope they treated me the same way. When it worked, it worked well, but when it didn't, it was a disaster.

The first problem came when I drilled into an old lead pipe concealed in one of the walls. The water pressure was so strong it was as if I'd turned on a fire hose. I quickly turned off the mains water valve to the flat, but it didn't make any difference: water kept spurting from the pipe. It turned out the pipe was supplying water to the flat upstairs. Under a stone in the front garden was a piece of old terracotta pipe, which was just wide enough to get my arm down. At the bottom of it was a stopcock to turn the water off to the whole house. I lay down and pushed my arm into the hole. I could just reach it with the tips of my fingers. But just as I started to turn it the head came off in my hand. I ran down to the street, but the council had recently resurfaced the pavement and had tarmacked over all the stopcocks on the path. Water was now pouring out of the room into the hallway and was starting to cascade down the steps into the front garden. Unless I turned it off soon, I was going to flood the entire flat. Thank God it was a ground-floor flat. A flood on a higher floor would have affected anything below. I grabbed a spade and started manically digging around the hole. I must have shifted almost a ton of earth in less than five minutes. The sweat poured off my forehead and ran into my eyes. I was covered in mud, lying in a hole a metre underground, with a pair of pincer pliers, trying to turn the tiny tip of metal that was protruding from the stopcock. When I finally succeeded in turning it off, my heart was beating so fast I thought it was going to explode out of my chest. I lay there for at least ten minutes trying to catch my breath. Fortunately, Judith wasn't there. She had left that morning to go to an audition in Chichester, so she never knew how close I came to flooding her flat.

The next crisis came when Big Pete tripped while he was plastering the ceiling. The plywood he was standing on flipped up and he went flying. Twenty stone came crashing down and he ended up wedged between two joists. I didn't think we would be able to get him out. He was all right, a bit bruised, but he hadn't broken any bones. He had, however, knocked out one of his front teeth. I found it underneath a floorboard, next to some old mouse droppings. 'Have you got any superglue?' he asked, washing it under the tap.

'What for?' I replied.

'To stick it back in.'

'Are you serious?'

'Yes. I don't do dentists,' he said, rooting around in my tool-box. That was what he was like. He stuck his tooth back in and got on with it. Health and safety was for wimps. Big Pete, Dale and Ryan were old-school tradesmen. They saw health and safety as an irritation, dreamed up by pencil-pushing pricks who didn't know anything about the practicalities of working on a building site. Chris, Fi and I saw it differently, so, in hindsight, it was inevitable that there would be an explosion at some point. Chris started it. He took health and safety very seriously. He wouldn't step onto the bottom of a stepladder unless someone had a foot on it, and he never knew when to keep his mouth shut. 'By rights, I should report you for that,' he said one morning as we were making our morning brew. It was never a good idea to threaten Big Pete, especially early in the morning. 'You what?' said Big Pete, walking towards him menacingly. 'Report me? Who to?' he said, squaring up to him.

'All I'm saying is you shouldn't use my bucket as a toilet. That's all.'

'Where was I supposed to go? Unless you haven't noticed there's no bloody khazi!'

'That's my fault,' I said, interrupting, trying to calm things down. 'I took it out yesterday. I should have put it back in, so everyone could use it this morning.'

'That's right. You should have. It's against regulations to not have a toilet on site.'

'Why don't you shove your fucking regulations up your arse?' said Big Pete, grabbing him by the throat.

'All I'm saying is it's disgusting to use my bucket.'

You had to give it to him; Chris wasn't frightened. He stood his ground, even when I thought Big Pete was going to punch his lights out. 'I cleaned it out, didn't I?' said Big Pete, justifying himself.

'Look, let go of him. He doesn't mean it. Do you Chris?' I said forcefully. 'It's my fault. I was held up at the plumbing merchant this morning and Big Pete had a skinful last night.'

Big Pete let him go and Chris quietly started packing up his tools.

'I'm sorry I can't work like this,' he said, walking out the door.

'Great. Now what are we going to do?' I said, running after him. I spent the rest of the day being Chris's therapist, hearing some things, in the course of six long hours, that I wish hadn't. I finally convinced him to return, on the understanding that he would never have to work with Big Pete again. The next day was my son's parent-teacher meeting at The Royal Ballet School, so I gave Ryan the keys and left Chris in charge.

The next morning, Jo woke up chewing a wasp. She had a real love-hate relationship with The Royal Ballet School. She loved the kudos, but hated the reality of it, and that morning she was particularly irritable. She'd spent most of the previous night making mental lists. 'I'm going to give them a piece of my mind,' she said, encouraging me to get ready. 'It's child abuse the way they are pushing him, that's what it is.' She glared at me. 'You're not wearing that.'

'Why not?'

'Because I want to make a good impression. You're not wearing jeans. Put your suit on.'

'I thought you hated them.'

'I do, but I don't want them to look down on us. Anyway, we're meeting his ballet teacher, then there's going to be a performance in the Pavlova Suite. Jeans just aren't appropriate,' she said, scurrying into the kitchen to make herself a cup of Moment of Calm herbal infusion.

When we arrived, we were escorted past the life-sized statue of Margot Fonteyn into the Grand Salon, where all the pictures of the royal family are. It was all very carefully choreographed. Everything was designed to reassert just how lucky we were that they had chosen our child. We were given tea and biscuits, and none of the parents talked to each other. The Royal Ballet School ruled by fear. From the moment we agreed to send our son there, his education and all his dreams were firmly in their hands. They had assessments every year and kicked out anyone who they didn't feel was up to scratch. They were ruthless. It was absolutely terrifying.

We soon learnt that the best thing to do was to say nothing and keep our heads down, because if we didn't, we probably wouldn't be at the next parent-teacher meeting. But none of that mattered because Jo was intent on giving them a piece of her mind! A few days earlier Oli had called us in tears and told us that they were forcing him to dance all day with splints threaded through his fingers and they regularly made him jump until he almost passed out. Jo was furious. Oli desperately pleaded with us not to say anything, but Jo was determined. His ballet teacher was a small, psychotic man who was better suited to Broadmoor than being a ballet teacher. We took our place in the queue and waited to be called in. I was nervous about what was about to transpire. Then just as our turn was about to come, my phone rang. Jo frowned at me as if to say, 'Don't you dare take that,' but I could see it was Fi. Fi never called me unless it was an emergency, so I ignored Jo and took the call.

'Ryan hasn't turned up. Dale tried to climb the fence, but it collapsed and now he's struggling to breathe. I've called an ambulance. It's on its way, but he's unconscious and it doesn't look good. Chris turned up a few minutes ago, but left as soon as he saw Big Pete. Basically, we can't get in, so we're all going to knock it on the head for today,' she said, leaving a short pause for me to reply: 'Okay, look, I'm just going in to a meeting. Can I call you back in ten minutes?'

'You can call me back if you like, but none of us will be here. Where's the bitch who owns the place? She must have some keys, surely?'

'She's not a bitch, she's an actress and she's at an audition in Chichester.'

'Well, tell her to get her bitch arse back here, otherwise I can't put the fuse board in until next week.'

'Is Dale okay? He's slightly asthmatic. Has he got his inhaler?' Jo was now staring at me like she was about to spontaneously combust. 'Fi, I've got to go. I'll call you back.' I quickly texted Ryan, 'Where the fuck are you?' and then took my seat next to Jo, but all I could think about was Dale.

'Hi,' I said, sitting down opposite Oli's psycho ballet teacher, who began telling us: 'He is progressing well, but he still needs to work on his lines. His arabesques are coming on, as are his pirouettes, but he needs more extension in his pliés. His hands are still a problem, so we've taken to using sticks to help to ingrain the position as quickly as possible. His flexibility is still very good, but he's growing quickly at the moment and he really needs to bulk up. The smaller ones have an advantage in this area, so we've put him on protein shakes and have given him a strict weights routine, nothing too rigorous, we don't want him to damage his knees,' he said, laughing, then suddenly looking deadly serious. 'We are still monitoring his urine and we're keeping an eye on his sugar intake. Obviously, the assessments are coming up. It will be down to how he performs on the day. I understand Darcey Bussell and Carlos Acosta are going to be judges this year. I should let you know that the headmaster has offered two places to the winners of the Prix de Lausanne and the Youth America Grand Prix competitions, so two boys and two girls are almost certainly going to have to go. Obviously, I can't make any promises, but as long as he continues to work hard, he might make it. Last year, seven out of the ten boys were assessed out. Do you have any questions?'

I looked at Jo as if to say, 'Go on then.'

'No, we'd just like to thank you for everything that you're doing,' she said, standing up to shake his hand.

'What the fuck was that?' I said as soon as we were outside. 'I thought you were going to give him a piece of your mind!'

'I know. I just felt so frightened. I don't want them to kick him out because of me. I'd never forgive myself.'

'Did you see the way he laughed, then suddenly changed? The guy is a psycho. He would have been kicked out of the SS for cruelty!'

'I know, but what can we do?'

'So, from now on, we're just going to shut up and let them do whatever they want to make him into the dancer he wants to be.'

'I guess so.'

'Even if it's bordering on child abuse?'

'What can we do? He wants to be here.'

'Okay,' I said, walking off to call Fi.

'Dale's been rushed into A&E,' she began. 'Big Pete's fucked off and says he's not coming back if Chris is there. Ryan has just turned up with the key, smelling like a brewery, and is making a hell of a mess notching the joists. I'm just about to change the fuse board, so don't worry, I'll see you tomorrow,' she said, putting down the phone.

Jo and I made our way down to the Pavlova Studio and waited for all the other parents to finish their meetings. 'Why doesn't anyone talk to each other?' I said under my breath.

'Because they know that their child is constantly being compared to ours,' said Jo, looking over at one of the other couples, who looked even more terrified than we did. 'It brings the worst out in people. They put us in a situation where we all know our child only gets what he wants if he's better than theirs. It's just awful.'

'I told you I could wear jeans. Look, *he's* wearing jeans.'

'Shut up! He looks awful.'

'What happens if he gets assessed out?'

'He'd be devastated. Then we'd have to find him another school. I suspect it's almost impossible to find one straight away, so he'll have to come back here to finish the next two terms.'

'But everyone here will know that he's been kicked out.'

'I know. But they don't care. They want the best and they don't care who they hurt in the process.'

'You could say they're preparing them for a ruthless and insecure world.'

'I'm sure that's how they spin it.'

'Maybe the sooner they get used to it, the better.'

'True, but it doesn't exactly encourage the parents to talk to each other, does it?'

'Mind you, on the plus side, if he is assessed out, we would get to see him every day.'

'That's true.'

'And we would know that he wasn't being physically abused by a sadistic psychopath armed with splints.'

'That's also true.'

'And we could afford to go on holiday.'

'Okay, don't get carried away. We don't want him to be assessed out!'

'No. Of course not. He'd be devastated. But our life would be better.'

'Stop it. Look, here comes his teacher. We're so looking forward to the performance,' said Jo, as he opened the door to the Pavlova Studio and showed us to our seats.

'You really showed him that time,' I said quietly, sitting down next to her.

'Shut up, I still hate him. I just don't want him to know it.'

'That makes me feel slightly insecure.'

'Why?'

'Because you're so convincing when you lie.'

'Oh, don't worry. I openly hate you, you bastard. Now shut up, it's about to start, and don't fall asleep.'

* * * *

When I got back to Judith's the next day, I discovered that Ryan had completely butchered the joists. I called the hospital and was told that Dale had had a heart attack and wouldn't be able to work for at least three months. Big Pete's tooth fell out again, and he swallowed it, so he begrudgingly went to the dentist and was told he needed two root canals and several implants, so he was going to be off for the next week. On the plus side, Fi had rewired the flat and changed the fuse board. Chris had started building the new kitchen and had made a start on the wardrobes in the bedroom.

Two weeks later, Dale collapsed at home and died on his way to hospital. It was a very sad day, and we all had far too much to drink in The Faltering Fullback in Finsbury Park. We sent him off in style and, when I left, I burst into tears and cried all the way home. I found out that night that he had a picture of Geoffrey Boycott above his bed. That made me smile.

The next day, Big Pete told me he had been offered a six-month job in an office block in Farringdon, so, from then on, it was just Ryan, Chris and me. Then Judith got back from Chichester, and all hell broke loose. The day after she got back, she was invited to audition for a part in *Fiddler on the Roof* in the West End. She had played the part before in a touring production, so it was no surprise when she got the role. This meant we had to get everything finished before opening night, which was in two weeks' time, so Chris and I both worked all the hours to get it done. Ryan begrudgingly worked until five o'clock, and made such a big deal about it, I couldn't wait for him to leave. We eventually finished it on the day of the premiere. When I got home that night, I walked in the front door and collapsed into my favourite armchair.

'Did you finish it?' said Jo, bringing me a glass of wine.

'Yes, literally as she was leaving to go to the theatre.'

'Is she pleased?'

'Yes, and she's already paid me.'

'That's great.'

'Oh, and look, she gave me these.'

'Are these the house seats?'

'I think so. Chris wasn't really interested so he gave me his ticket.'

'It's the school holidays next week.'

'I know, I thought you might like to take him. He's never seen *Fiddler on the Roof* on stage.'

'Are you sure you don't mind?'

'Yes, he'll love it. Tradition. Tradition,' I said, putting both my arms in the air and waving them about. 'Oh, I checked my bank balance after she transferred the funds, and I've got the money for next term's school fees.'

'Really, that's brilliant! You know that means they'll put them up next year, don't you?'

'No, why?'

'Because we've earned more money.'

'Yes, to pay for the bloody school fees.'

'I know, but they don't care.'

'So, you're telling me that for the next eight years we're going to be stuck with ever-increasing school fees?'

'I'm afraid so,' she said, taking a sip of her wine.

★ ★ ★ ★

The following week, Jo took Oli to see Judith in *Fiddler on the Roof* and, when it finished, they went round to the stage door. Judith walked out and recognised him instantly. 'You're Nick's boy, aren't you?' she said, signing his programme. 'Your dad's built me a great bathroom, he even made me a vanity unit with lights round it, just like the one I've got in my dressing room here. Where is he? I thought he'd be with you?'

'He gave the tickets to us,' said Jo, introducing herself.

'You could die from such a man,' she said, quoting Golda. 'He told me you're mad for the theatre. Come in, I'll introduce you to the rest of the cast.' Judith grabbed Oli's hand and took him inside. He was in seventh heaven. When they came out, Judith turned to Jo and said, 'He's born for the theatre that one.'

From that moment on, The Royal Ballet School was just a means to an end; musical theatre was what he really wanted to do. It always had been. Musicals were where his heart truly lay. I'm pleased that he made it all the way through The Royal Ballet School before he jumped ship to focus on his real goal. In the meantime, Jo and I continued to feed his passion – Jo was right, every time we earned the money to pay the school fees, the bastards put them up – but, with the little money we had left, we took him to the theatre, and now he's seen almost everything. He's still just as obsessed as he was when he watched 'Jophus' all those years ago. He is over six foot four now and he can still put his legs over his head. Last year, for his birthday, we took him to see *9 to 5* at the Savoy Theatre. When we got there, the security guard asked him how he was. Then, downstairs in the foyer, one of the ushers asked him if he would like 'his usual' in the interval. 'What's going on? How come all these people know you?' I said, as I made my way down the aisle.

'Oh, that's because of *Dreamgirls*,' he replied, nonchalantly.

'What do you mean?' I said, still somewhat perplexed.

'I used to sneak over and see it after school. There's an app I've got, if you happen to be available ten minutes before the show starts, they sell you tickets for next to nothing.'

'Really?'

'It helps if you are on your own, because it's usually individual seats. I used to hang around at school, then come down here just before it was about to start.'

'And the school allowed you to do that?'

'No, not really, but it seemed like too good an opportunity to miss.'

'How many times did you see it?'

'Seventeen. That's why they all know me.' When we walked out of the theatre that night, it occurred to me that most parents probably don't worry about their child's theatre habit. It dawned on me that we are all a merry band of misfits, wandering around in the dark, trying to find our way, with only our passions to guide us. 'What did you think of the show?' I said, crossing The Strand. 'I loved it, Dad,' he said, putting his arm around me as the Number 91 bus brushed up against the pavement and opened its doors, inviting us home.

3

Jesus

As well as plumbing, I also started managing some property in London for friends and clients who were living abroad. Lucy was a very accomplished costume designer. Consequently, she spent a lot of time travelling, so I looked after her house when she was away. She was always asking me to do bits and bobs and on this particular day she wanted me to install a new radiator in her study, so I texted her the day before to check it was still going to be okay and my phone pinged almost immediately.

'Yes that's great. I'm not there, but you can let yourself in. I've got a keypad now on the front door. I'll text you the number. Help yourself to tea and coffee. Just text me when you're done and let me know how much I owe you and I'll transfer the money.'

'Okay. Are you going to be contactable, in case I need to talk to you about anything?'

'No, not really. I'm in LA. What time are you planning to do it? I'm eight hours behind, so from about 4 p.m. to 6 p.m. UK time I'll be available, but after that I'm in back-to-back meetings.'

'Fair enough. I'll text you when it's done.'

'Thank you so much. The number for the door is 2001. The year Lulu was born.'

The next morning I got up early and sat quietly on my own listening to the tranquilising tick of my Vienna regulator clock, psyching myself up for the day ahead. Jo came through just as I was about to leave and started telling me what she was doing that day, but I wasn't really listening.

'I'm meeting Mary for a walk later. We're going up the Parkland Walk.'

'Great, see you later,' I said, walking out the door.

Ten minutes later, I picked up Ryan and drove straight to my plumbing merchant. Ryan had been out of action for a few days. He didn't tell me why, but his arm was in a sling and he stunk of TCP. Every now and again, Ryan would go AWOL, then he'd turn up several days later, stinking of booze and occasionally carrying an injury. I sometimes wondered if he was a member of the IRA. I knew he'd had to leave Ireland in a hurry and that he was a staunch republican, but whenever 'The Troubles' came up in conversation he completely clammed up. He'd recently moved into a hovel in Hackney. His landlord was one of the most notorious drug dealers in East London, who had recently been in all the papers because he set his dog on a couple of crackheads. Ryan had been behaving strangely ever since; he was absolutely terrified and Ryan didn't scare easily. His landlord's dog was a huge American pit bull called Brutus. He was the canine equivalent of a great white shark, and Ryan was petrified of pooches.

'So, what have we got on today?' he said, slipping his arm out of the sling and hiding it behind his back as he got into the van. He immediately wound the window down, to try to hide the invasive smell of alcohol mixed with TCP that was seeping out of every pore.

'Good night, was it?'

'Yeah, it was okay.'

'What's up with your arm?'

'Nothing, it's fine.'

'Good, because we've got a lot on today. We've got to fix a toilet first thing, then we've got to fix a couple of taps up in Highgate and then we've got to change a radiator over in Stroud Green.'

'What's the rad?'

'Can't remember. I looked at it ages ago.'

'Watch the van,' I said, pulling up outside the plumbing merchant. John, the shop assistant, was standing outside smoking a cigarette. His hair was cropped short and he'd grown an enormous pair of sideburns. 'All right, John,' I greeted him. 'What's with the bugger bars?'

'I had to shave my head, so I thought I'd grow it on my face instead!'

'You look like a Victorian butcher!'

'Thanks.'

'Why did you have to shave your scalp?'

'The missus found a growth. Look, I had to have it removed a few days ago,' he said, leaning forward to show me the scar on the top of his head.

'Jesus, what was it?'

'I was growing a horn.'

'What? Like a unicorn?' I said, laughing.

'Yeah, the other day I got the missus to check my arse, in case I was growing a tail!'

'Big Pete told me he saw you down The Dutch House with half of Tower Hamlets up your hooter!'

John laughed, stubbed out his cigarette and went back into the shop. 'So, what do you want?' he said, walking round to the other side of the counter.

'Half a pound of mince, two dozen sausages and a free-range chicken.'

'Very funny.'

'I need a close coupling kit.'

'Don't we all,' he said, laughing.

'Some doughnuts [washers]. I don't know what size, so give us a selection and I'll take that vertical rad I ordered last week.'

'Liam, he's taking The Beast,' John called across to his assistant.

'Best of luck with that bastard,' said Liam from the other side of the shop.

'You'll have to empty your van first, otherwise you'll fuck the suspension,' said John, pointing to it.

'Really?'

'I'm not joking. Liam and I brought it in. It's over there. Check it out. I swear that radiator weighs at least 200 kilograms, and that's without any bloody water in it. I hope it's going on a solid wall.'

'Can you give me a hand with it? Ryan's done his arm in and he has to keep an eye on the van.'

'Liam will give you an 'and.'

'Will I, fuck!' said Liam from the far side of the shop.

'Anything else?' said John, ignoring him.

'Yeah, give me some nice marinated ribs and a couple of slices of your best bacon!'

'Very funny. Here, give me a squiggle,' he said, handing me the invoice.

'I'll settle up tomorrow.'

'No worries,' he said, handing me my bag full of bits.

★ ★ ★ ★

Four hours later, Ryan and I finally arrived outside Lucy's house with 'The Beast' strapped to the roof of my van. 'There's no way we'll get it done today,' said Ryan as he got out of the van and started to undo the fastening straps. 'It's far too late!'

It was getting close to the time when Ryan's alcohol levels needed to be topped up. He started fidgeting, his hands began to shake and the smell of stale Guinness surrounded him, permeating his T-shirt and filling the air with the stench of stout. 'Look, can you stop fucking complaining!' I told him. 'It won't take us that long. I'll go and open the door.'

'I bet it's going on the top floor,' he mumbled under his breath as I made my way up the steps.

'It's not, actually. It's going on the first floor, in her study.'

'So that means we're going to have to drain the whole bloody house.'

'No, we'll drain it through the valves as far as the first floor.'

'Bet you don't know where the filling loop is?'

'Yes, I do! It's in the kitchen. Can you stop being so negative? You're doing my head in. We're changing a bloody radiator, not solving world peace!'

I walked up to the front door and entered the code into the keypad. The latch retracted and I pushed the door open. As I turned around to go and get the radiator, a huge albino dog came bounding up the stairs and launched itself at me. I quickly closed the door and I heard it crash against the other side.

'Jesus. What the fuck was that?' said Ryan, walking towards me. 'There's a huge dog in there, isn't there?'

'No,' I lied, as it started barking.

'Yes there is. I just saw it. You can fucking forget it. I'm not going in there. No way.'

'It's nothing, it's just a little lapdog. Wouldn't hurt a fly. I just don't know what its name is, that's all. I'm going to text Lucy to find out.'

'That didn't look like a lapdog to me!'

'So, you saw it then?'

'Just the outline.'

'What was it?'

'I don't know, but it ain't no lapdog. I don't care what it is, I'm not going in there. I hate dogs. One bit me when I was a kid. Bloody thing ripped my left nipple off.'

'All right, give me a moment.'

'Didn't she tell you she had a dog?'

'No, it must have slipped her mind.'

'Slipped her mind! Oh, by the way, there's a huge hound in the house. He's friendly enough, if he knows you, which he doesn't, in which case he might tear your fucking face off!'

'All right, I'll deal with this. Go and roll yourself another fag. Anyway, it's not faces he's after, it's nipples. Right nipples. He collects them. Extra juicy!'

Ryan gave me a dirty look and went to sulk in the van.

'Hi Lucy,' I texted, 'Sorry to bother you so early, but what's the name of your dog? All the best, Nick.'

'Jesus.'

'His name?'

'Yes.'

'As in Christ?'

'Yes.'

'Is he good-natured?'

'Yes. He can be.'

'What does that mean?'

'No, he's a sweetheart. There are some treats just inside the front door. Give him one of them and he'll be your best friend. Hope it goes okay. I'm about to go in to a breakfast meeting, so I'll be incommunicado from now on. Best of luck, don't show any fear and keep one hand on your genitals at all times!' (Followed by a smiley-face emoji.)

I punched the code into the keypad and slowly pushed the door open with my foot.

'Okay, Jesus.' The dog barked ferociously and stood defiantly on the other side of the door.

'It's okay, Jesus, it's only me,' I continued.

'You sound like you're going to a bloody prayer meeting,' shouted Ryan from the van.

The dog's lips peeled back to expose its front teeth.

'For fuck's sake,' I said, closing the door quickly. 'It's a fucking wolf!'

'Let's call it quits,' said Ryan. 'We can't work with a wolf in the house, it's a dangerous animal!'

'Always looking for any bloody excuse, aren't you? We're doing the bloody job. Just give me a few minutes to figure this out.'

Two minutes later, I tied a red bandana around my head to keep my hair out of my eyes. I grabbed an old piece of lead pipe out of the back of the van and wrapped a towel around my left arm. I looked like Axl Rose on the *Appetite for Destruction* tour. I walked back towards the house. 'Okay, Jesus, back off!' I said, opening the front door. The dog barked and snarled as I pushed the door slowly open with my foot. 'I'm coming in. Whether you like it or not!' Jesus's lips curled back and saliva dripped from the corners of his mouth. He looked like a rabid albino Alsatian. 'If you bite me, it will be more than this lead pipe you'll have to deal with. I'll get medieval on your arse,' I said, slowly moving towards him. 'I've got a blow-torch in the van. You'll think the crucifixion was a bloody birthday present! Now back off! I'm coming in!' The dog gradually retreated and stood there snarling at me as I slowly reached for the treats. I quickly grabbed a handful and threw them down the stairs towards the basement. The dog jumped up, but missed them in mid-air and quickly turned and ran down the stairs after them. At that moment I felt like I was in a Vietnam movie. I suddenly started running after it shouting, 'Ahhhhh,' waving my weapon as if I was securing a settlement in the jungle just outside Saigon. The dog ran into the kitchen with its tail between its legs and I quickly shut the door behind it. I walked out of that house as if I'd just freed a Vietnamese village. 'It's okay, it's over. You get the front, I'll get the back. Let's get this baby inside,' I said, as if I'd just been given a top-secret mission to terminate a rogue colonel's command in a Cambodian hideout.

Half an hour later, Ryan and I were still arguing about how we were going to proceed. 'There's no way we'll get this done today. We're going to have to come back,' he said, rolling himself yet another cigarette.

'We can't come back,' I told him, 'We're starting a bloody bathroom tomorrow! Okay, how about we move it along a bit so the left brackets screw directly into the upright and then we use toggle bolts on the other side to brace behind the board?'

'No way, it's too heavy. It'll rip them straight out of the wall.'

'Okay, how about we bridge between the uprights with some wood on top of the existing wall and then we hang it onto that?'

'That could work. But it'll push it out of the wall.'

'Only a bit, and that shouldn't matter.'

'You better check with her first.'

'Okay, I'll drop her a text.'

'Hi Lucy,' I tapped out. 'Just realised the wall you want the new radiator to go on is a stud wall, so it isn't strong enough to take the weight. I can either open up the wall, put some wood in, re-board it, re-plaster it and redecorate it, then put the new radiator in or I can plant some wood onto the outside of the wall to strengthen it and hang the radiator off that. The second option will obviously mean the radiator is a little bit further off the wall, but it will mean I can do it today and it will obviously be a hell of a lot cheaper. I don't think you'll really notice it when it's painted. Let me know what you would like me to do.'

A message came back almost immediately.

'Whatever you think. Can't speak. In a meeting.'

'Okay, she agrees,' I told Ryan. 'I've got some wood in the van. You measure it and I'll cut it. It's almost drained down now. We're going to be fine, ye of little faith.'

Several hours later, we had almost finished fitting the new radiator. Ryan was suffering from serious withdrawal symptoms: he was sweating profusely and his hands were shaking so much he could hardly hold a spanner. 'You'd better go and fill it up,' he said, sitting down on the top step of the stairs, knowing full well that to fill the system I'd have to go into the kitchen, where the dog was. 'Okay,' I said, slightly apprehensively, as I started wrapping the towel tightly round my left arm. I felt like I was rejoining my platoon after some R and R and now there was a whole division of Charlie concealed in those kitchen cupboards needing to be dealt with.

'You're kidding me! You better not let it out. I mean it. If it comes anywhere near me, I'm out of here!' said Ryan, as I picked up the pipe.

'Don't worry, he's going outside,' I said, as I made my way down the stairs.

I opened the kitchen door, but there was no sign of him, so I pushed it open a little further with my foot. Jesus was asleep on the far side of the kitchen with a plastic baby's arm in his mouth. The rest of the doll had been shredded and lay scattered all over the floor. There was a foot next to the fridge and its head had been flung high into the air and had landed next to the hob.

'Okay, Jesus, it's time to go outside,' I said, walking over to the back door without taking my eyes off him. The dog growled, but he didn't move. Fortunately, the key was in the lock, so I quickly turned it and opened the door. The dog paused for a moment, then suddenly jumped to its feet and came careering across the kitchen towards me. I withdrew my weapon and waited for Jesus to get within range. Then I turned and tossed some treats out into the garden. He charged past me and bounded through the bamboo borders as smoke from next door's barbecue hung over the garden. I was at the mouth of the Nung River. The paddling pool was covered in a thin film of gasoline, the half-chewed action man was saying, 'If I say it's safe to surf, it's safe to surf.' The soiled sandpit was the bombed-out beach, the smoke was fumes from flares, and the camouflaged climbing frame at the end of the garden was Charlie's headquarters. There was a burnt-out firepit in front of me and the scorched yellow Astroturf was covered in burst beach balls and decapitated dolls, all proof that I was in a war zone. Jesus appeared out of the shredded shrubbery at the far end of the garden, his lips drawn back, blood dripping from his canines as he bounded back towards me. He intended to terminate my command. Terminate it with extreme prejudice.

Just then, Ryan called to me from upstairs, 'Have you started filling it yet?' he shouted, and just like that, I was immediately transported back to being a plumber, not far from the Arsenal stadium. I quickly closed the door, went over to the boiler and started to fiddle with the filling loop, while Jesus jumped up outside the door, frothing at the mouth, jabbing his teeth into the joinery.

An hour later, we finished and I started to put my tools away, while Ryan went outside for a fag. 'Where do you want to be dropped?' I asked him.

'Down the road – I'm seeing a man about a dog,' he said, wiping his brow with his sleeve, smearing dirt across his forehead. At that moment, he had joined me on patrol. We scouted round the house, checking for Charlie, and then we left. 'That wasn't too bad. We did that in four-and-half hours. Not bad at all!'

'You're going to leave the dog in the garden then, are you?' said Ryan, getting into the passenger seat.

'Yes, I think so. Come to think of it, I didn't see it when I went down to the kitchen. Did you?'

'No.'

'Hang on, I'll just go and check.'

'It'll be fine, it's probably just asleep somewhere, having eaten a small child,' he said, licking his Rizla.

'I won't be long.' Ten minutes later I appeared in the doorway, white as a sheet. 'It's not there. It's completely disappeared!'

'What do you mean? It can't have.'

'It has. I'm telling you. It's not there. It must have got out.'

'Shit!'

'What the hell am I going to tell Lucy?' I asked him.

'Don't worry about it, it'll turn up.'

'Hi Lucy, the radiator's fine, but I've lost your dog. Fuck! It could be anywhere.'

'I'll tell you what. You go and check the house and I'll check out here. What's its name again?'

'Jesus.'

'Are you serious?'

'Honest to God.'

'What does it look like?'

'What?'

'I haven't seen it. You locked it away before I went in there, remember.'

'Jesus, Ryan! It looks like a fucking wolf! It looks like a German Shepherd that's been genetically modified to look a bit more Aryan.'

For the next ten minutes, Ryan walked up and down the road shouting, 'Jesus, Jesus. Come back, Jesus. Jesus, come back here,' in his pronounced Irish accent. All to no avail. When I came out of the house, I decided to come clean and texted Lucy:

'Hi Lucy, Please see attached a picture of your new radiator. Everything's fine and it's all working well. We had to put a couple of pieces of wood on the wall to help take the weight of it, but they're hardly visible. I let Jesus out to keep him out of the way and he seems to have completely disappeared. Is there anywhere we should go to look? Does he have any favourite places he might go? I'm so sorry, Lucy. I don't know what to say. We'll obviously keep looking, but can you please give me a ring as I'm starting to hyperventilate. I'm feeling like I've just inadvertently walked into the sequel of *An American Werewolf in London*! I'm really, really sorry! All the best, Nick.' An hour later, after we had both scoured the entire area, shouting, 'Jesus, where the fuck are you, Jesus!' we eventually arrived back at the house and decided to give up. Then I really started to panic. All sorts of crazy things kept racing through my mind: 'Was it my responsibility to look after her dog? I didn't even know she had a dog. What was she thinking keeping a fully-grown wolf in the house. She knew I was coming today.' I went back into the house to check one last time, then I took out my phone and started to write to Lucy:

'Hi Lucy, I'm afraid I've done everything I can to try to find him, but he's nowhere to be seen. Do you want me to call the police?'

Suddenly, the front door opened, and in leapt Jesus.

'Oh my God! Jesus! Where have you been!' I said, overcome with relief. The dog just stood there and looked at me. I quickly opened the door and saw a young woman walking down the street. 'Thank you so much,' I shouted out.

'I beg your pardon,' she said, somewhat perplexed, as she started walking away from me.

'Where did you find him? Jesus, I mean,' I said, running after her.

'What do you mean?' she said, looking at me as if I'd just told her I thought I was the son of God.

'The dog, where did you find him?' I asked.

'I didn't. He lives there.'

'Yes, I know. He escaped. I've been looking for him everywhere. I've been driving the streets, shouting, "Jesus, Jesus, where the hell are you, Jesus?".'

The young woman suddenly stopped and burst out laughing. 'Sorry,' she said, unable to stop giggling. 'I … picked him up about an hour ago … I'm Lucy's dog walker. I come every day to take him out for a walk. Sorry, I didn't know that there was anyone else in the house.'

'What! I've just spent the last hour trying to find him.'

'Oh, poor you! I'm so sorry.'

'Don't worry, I'm just so relieved. Aren't you scared, walking a dog like that?'

'Oh, he's a big softie really. Mind you, he did just almost eat a Pomeranian. He doesn't like small dogs. Or dogs that can't breathe properly. Other than that, he's good as gold.'

I took out my phone and wrote to Lucy. 'Hi Lucy, False alarm. No cause for concern. I've found Jesus! You didn't tell me you had a dog walker!'

Ryan was laughing when I got back to the van. 'Unbelievable! What is she doing with a dog like that?'

'Haringey home protection, I presume. No one's going to break in with that inside and, if they do, they'll soon scarper. It apparently just tried to pulverise a Pomeranian.'

'Where?'

'On the Parkland Walk. No wonder you don't see any cats round here, it's probably eaten them all.'

'Can you drop me down the bottom of the road?' said Ryan, closing the passenger door. 'I'm seeing some new digs tonight.'

'That's good,' I said, driving past a church with a sign on the wall saying, *Jesus loves you!* 'Yeah, right, he does, I'll get out here,' he said, opening the door as I pulled up at the junction. As he got out, a small piece of paper fell out of his pocket. I opened it and in the top right corner was a green phoenix, the tops of its wings etched in red. Above it were the words, 'Out of The Ashes Arose The' and beneath it was the word 'Provisionals' in green and red Gaelic script. It was addressed to Rian O'Brien care of Darragh Docherty. The letter was in Gaelic so I couldn't read it, but Darragh Docherty was Ryan's old landlord. I quickly folded it up and put it back on the seat next to me.

When I got home, Jo was sitting watching *Peppa Pig* with the kids.

'How did it go?' she said, as Daddy Pig started jovially jumping into muddy puddles.

'You don't want to know.'

'Why?'

'Lucy's got a wolf called Jesus. I put it in the garden because Ryan's terrified of dogs and it disappeared. I spent an hour circumnavigating Stroud Green shouting, "Jesus, Jesus, where are you, Jesus." Ryan's Irish accent added to it somehow, only to find out Lucy's got a dog walker. She'd taken the dog and not told us. Ryan's been a bolshie bastard all day and there's a ten-to-one chance that he's a terrorist. Other than that, everything's fine.' Just then my phone pinged. 'That'll be Lucy,' I said.

'What does it say?' said Jo, looking over my shoulder.

'Thanks for letting me know. So sorry, should have told you about the dog and the dog walker. Totally slipped my mind. Anyway, it's about time you found Jesus,' with lots of laughing emojis.

'Oh, I'm so sorry,' said Jo, laughing.

'Anyway, how was your day?' I said, going down into the cellar to take off my plumbing trousers.

'Just the usual, really. Mum paid the wrong part of the invoice again. She seems to only pay the VAT. I keep getting calls from people saying, "Thank you for paying the government, but would you mind paying for the work as well!" I went for a walk with Mary. She was in a right state. A huge white dog appeared out of nowhere and went for her Pomeranian. She only just managed to pick it up in time. There was a young girl who was supposed to be in charge of it, but she just kept saying, "Jesus, Jesus," then it ran off. It never occurred to us that might actually be its name!'

4

Checkmate

The older I get, the more I think life is like a game of chess. No matter how much I plan ahead, I always end up spontaneously reacting to what's in front of me. My actions make me think I'm in control, but I'm not – not really. No matter how hard I try to predict what's coming next, I can never be sure, so all I can do is play the percentages. But sometimes, the most unlikely things really do happen.

Jo's father was a keen chess player. He taught Oli to play when he was six and he picked it up pretty quickly. There was a chess tournament coming up at his primary school, so he signed up for it. His grandpa had taught him a couple of opening moves; no one knew them, so he won. That meant he was put forward to compete in The London Junior Chess Championship. So now, as well as taking him to multiple dance classes, we had to ferry him all over London to play chess. Grandparents, they're great, aren't they?

At this time, I was compartmentalising my life. I had a box in my brain for work, and another for family. I tried not to mix them up. Plumbing was hard enough without also having to get my kids to all their extra-curricular activities. But sometimes my parental responsibilities had to take priority. Most of the time I could rely on Jo to juggle her job whilst also dealing with the kids and our ageing parents. She was brilliant at it. Unlike me, she was a natural multitasker. Jo could talk to lawyers while she was doing the laundry. She could drive our daughter to dance classes while explaining to her dad how to use a dongle. She could do both our tax returns while simultaneously suing someone for copyright infringement. She was a dynamo. She had the patience of a saint and the juggling ability of an acrobat. So, when she asked me to cover the kids, because she had back-to-back meetings in Mayfair, I couldn't say no. It was my turn to hold the fort. Unfortunately, my brain worked differently. I could do only one thing at a time and if things collided, I easily fell apart.

All I had to do that day was take my daughter to her cranial therapy appointment and then take my son to his chess tournament. I didn't know what cranial therapy was, but there was apparently no way she could miss it. From what I gathered, someone placed their hands on her head, chanted for half an hour and then charged us fifty quid. It all sounded a bit biblical to me, but Jo swore it helped her with her anxiety. She was only three. Who has anxiety when they are three? But there was no point arguing; if Jo thought our daughter needed biblical redemption, then that was what she was going to get. Initially, I was fairly laid back about it. I did my risk assessment, and it didn't seem too difficult, so I nonchalantly said, 'No problem.' Nothing could faze me. I was firmly in control.

I had only two jobs to do that day: I had to fix a leak in a pet shop in Palmers Green, then put a worktop into a kitchen in Kentish Town. The cranial appointment wasn't until three o'clock, so, as long as I was back home by half past two, I'd be fine. But some jobs are just jinxed. There's nothing you can do about it. In hindsight, I should probably have taken the day off; I should have known that I wouldn't be able to fit it all in. Just because Jo could juggle, it didn't mean that I could. I frequently felt as if I was presiding over a looming calamity, that I was one step away from catastrophe. And asking me to multitask was all it took for my whole house of cards to come crashing down.

I left early to beat the traffic. Ryan turned up on crutches. He had been up all night drinking and was still pissed. 'I fell off a wall,' he slurred. He smelt like a distillery and had come straight from A&E. So, when we got to where we were going, I told him to go and get some breakfast and I went to fix the leak in the pet shop myself. When I opened the door, a woman with lots of tattoos was dropping a frozen fish into a tank full of piranhas. They stripped it to the bone in a few seconds.

'Hi I'm Petra. Are you the plumber?' she said, looking at my tool-box. 'The pipe split,' she said, pointing to the pipe feeding the valve on the top of the tank. She was an interesting-looking woman with big, brooding eyes and long, black hair that she hooked behind her ears.

'Surprisingly, working with flesh-eating fish isn't something I come across often,' I said, putting down my tool-box. I had a small cut on my right hand; whenever I gripped anything, it opened up. It had been like that for months because it never had enough time to heal. I turned the water off, held the valve with my left hand, then attached the pipe slice onto the pipe and started to turn it to cut the pipe. The cut on my hand opened up and a small drop of blood fell into the water. My plan was to remove the valve, replace the pipe, then reattach it. It should have been pretty straightforward, but the copper was thin. My pipe slice cut straight through it, catching me unawares. As it gave way, I dropped it into the tank. Without thinking, I plunged my hand into the water to try to retrieve it. The fish swam quickly towards it. I suddenly realised what I had done and imagined them stripping my hand to the bone. For a split second, I froze. One of them opened its mouth and sped towards my fingers. I felt like I was watching it in slow motion, my bleeding hand magnified by the glass. I pulled it out just as they were about to attack.

'You're lucky,' she said, dropping another frozen fish into the tank.

'Not a single nip,' I said, wiping my hand on my T-shirt as they devoured the dead fish. 'You can keep the pipe slice,' I said, pointing to the tool at the bottom of the tank.

'Are you sure?'

'Yes, I don't fancy putting my hand back in there to get it,' I said, grabbing a spanner out of my tool-box and attaching a new piece of pipe.

When I finished, I walked to the back of the shop.

'How much do I owe you?' she said, walking over to the till.

'Call it fifty quid,' I said, looking around. It was a strange place: full of lots of exotic pets that you wouldn't normally put together. There was a huge blue-and-yellow parrot sitting on a perch next to the till. Behind it was a cage of white rats with red eyes. One of them was running in its wheel as if its life depended on it.

'We used to keep them to feed to the snakes,' she said, pointing to a series of vivariums. Next to the rats was a series of fish tanks full of Japanese fighting fish. 'We used to feed them to the piranhas, but they're quite popular now. Here you go,' she said, handing me a cheque.

The name on the bottom of the cheque was Peter Papadopoulos.

'Is that your name?'

'No, it's my uncle's. This is his shop.'

'Is he Greek?'

'Yes, Greek Cypriot, actually. He left me some signed cheques.'

'Why? Where is he?'

'He's retired. He lets me live upstairs and, in return, I run the shop.'

'Sorry. Your uncle, who, if you don't mind me saying, has quite a lot of Ps in his name, left you some cheques to pay the plumber?'

'Yes, that's right,' she said, laughing.

'That's a lot of Ps!'

'Yes, I suppose it is. We also have a lot of parrots,' she said, walking across the room and opening a door. The room was full of birdcages of every shape and size. There must have been over twenty parrots in that room: African greys, hyacinth macaws, sulphur-crested cockatoos, sun conures ... you name it, they were all there. And every single one started squawking as soon as she opened the door.

At that moment, Ryan hobbled in carrying a McDonald's breakfast. 'Have you got the van keys?' he shouted. The squawking was so shrill it felt like someone was drilling into the back of my brain. Ryan looked like he was about to throw up. So I threw him the keys and he went to sit in the van.

'Parrots are what we're known for, the rest is just for show,' she shouted, closing the door.

'And the huge python?' I said, pointing to an enormous snake curled up in the corner of a vast vivarium at the back of the shop.

'He's not for sale. He's my uncle's. He's a Burmese. We think he's the largest snake in London. That's why we started keeping the rabbits,' she said, pointing out of the window. In the back garden, was a pen full of rabbits.

'You keep rabbits to feed your python?'

'Initially we did, but we don't feed them to him anymore. We buy frozen rabbits. Just like we don't feed fresh fish to the piranhas or live rats to our other snakes any more.'

'Wow,' I said, feeling slightly uncomfortable. 'Don't tell me your uncle's retired to the Peloponnese to grow pomegranates,' I said, joking.

'No, to Portugal to play golf,' she replied, smiling.

I imagined the mad menagerie of exotic pets she probably had upstairs. A boa constrictor in the bath, perhaps, or a Komodo dragon in the kitchen. When I got back to the van, Ryan was still eating his McDonald's. Ketchup was dripping from his chin.

'I reckon I've just been given a dodgy cheque,' I said, getting in. 'But we're on a tight schedule today and she's got too many dangerous animals in there to argue,' I continued, turning on the ignition. Ryan was still monosyllabic.

'Like what?' he said, showing me a mouthful of McMuffin.

'I'm going to call Chris, to check he's still okay to meet us at the next job.'

'Not Chris,' said Ryan, groaning as he inhaled his hash brown.

'I'm on my way to Wickes to get the worktop; I'll see you there in an hour,' I said as soon as Chris picked up the phone. The best way to deal with Chris was to get straight to the point.

'Funny you should say that,' he said. That was how he always started his sentences. Something told me he was about tell me a story. Half an hour was a short story for Chris. 'I was supposed to be working outside today, but I've just been rained off.' I could see he was going to tell me everything about everything. 'It's a curious job, really. It's a shed; well, more of a studio really. He's a musician, well, an engineer. He mixes music, did that Morcheeba album. He asked me to build him a recording studio at the back of his garden. He was going to get a prefab, but he changed his mind and now he's gone for something completely bespoke. It's quite cool, actually ...'

'That's great. I really appreciate you helping me out. I'll see you there in an hour,' I said, cutting him short and putting the phone down, before he started telling me which wood he was using and the size of the various screws.

'Not Chris,' slurred Ryan again, biting into his second sausage-and-egg McMuffin.

I drove straight to Wickes. When we got there, Jo called me in a right state. 'Mum's hosting the chavurah tonight. She wants me to help her set up the sandwiches.' Miriam, Jo's mum, had recently joined a group of reformed Jews. They met every Tuesday to talk about the Torah. Tonight they were supposed to be discussing what it meant to be Jewish. That was a recipe for disaster. Miriam and Jo disagreed about pretty much everything, especially religion. Jo's parents weren't orthodox Jews, but they did have separate plates for meat and dairy, and another set for Indian takeaways, because my father-in-law liked Tandoori king prawns. They were reformed Jews; they just weren't as reformed as Jo. I wasn't Jewish and, unlike her mother, Jo wasn't defined by her Jewishness. Most of our friends weren't Jewish. We weren't kosher. We celebrated Christmas and Easter, as well as Hanukkah and Passover. Our children were seriously religiously confused, but that was by design. Neither of us believed in any of it. We did an Easter-egg hunt after Passover. Our son told his teacher that we celebrated the birth of Jesus at Hanukkah. At Yom Kippur, he told a room full of Miriam's friends that he wasn't hungry (at the break of the fast) because Dad had cooked roast pork for lunch. Jo pretended to be interested to keep her mother happy, but she wasn't. We were secretly hoping that religious confusion would ultimately lead to both our children becoming secular like us. But Miriam had other ideas. She was determined that our kids would grow up to be Jewish, and she was doing everything she could to make this happen. Asking Jo to join the chavurah was just another roundabout way of trying to introduce more Judaism into our children's lives. Because we had a mixed marriage, we had to deal with the issues that often come to the surface when two cultures collide.

'I need you to bring the kids to Mum's. I'm going straight there from my meetings. She wants to show them off at the chavurah. It's sweet, she hasn't seen them in a month! But it's sweet.' I could tell that Miriam had been winding Jo up about not being Jewish enough, so I just nonchalantly said, 'No problem,' and put the phone down. That was an argument I definitely didn't want to be part of. Jo knew what her mother was up to; this was just another attempt to introduce more Judaism by stealth.

Ryan and I drove straight to Kentish Town. When we arrived, Chris was already there. He immediately started telling me a story about a kitchen he'd built in Bethnal Green. Ryan shoved a couple of cigarette butts into his ears and wandered off.

'That one needed two corners cut,' he said, as my eyes started to glaze over. 'I bought the jig. I got it from Toucan Tools. I don't use it much. It's nice to have a job that needs it. I've brought three jigsaws just in case. It really depends on the depth of the worktop and the size of the screws we're going to use …'

'Right, that's it. I'm sorry, Chris. I'm in a bit of a rush today,' I said, interrupting him. 'Can you get the other end of the worktop, Ryan's a bit worse for wear this morning,' I continued, untying the bungees on my roof-rack to take down the three-metre kitchen worktop, hoping it might stop him talking. 'Ryan, you get the doors.' The property was a three-storey converted townhouse, not far from Camden Market. Ryan rang the bell and the latch retracted. Post was piled up inside the front door and bikes were hanging from hooks in the corridor, making the communal area feel cramped. Ryan held the door open while Chris and I tried to manoeuvre the worktop up the stairs.

'The staircase is only 800 mm wide,' said Chris, measuring it with the trusty tape measure that he kept attached to his trousers at all times.

I imagined him hitching his tape measure to the waistband of his pyjamas, in case of any emergency midnight measuring. Who was I kidding? Chris didn't wear pyjamas. He slept in dungarees, smudged with wood stain, with pockets full of broken drill bits, short pencils and mildly pornographic pictures of women holding power tools.

'Where's it going?' he said, breaking my train of thought.

'The top floor.'

'The only way to get it up there will be up the front of the house.'

After fifteen minutes of trying to force it up the stairs, I had to concede that Chris was right. I left Ryan downstairs guarding the worktop. Chris went upstairs to introduce himself to my client and I went to hire a triple ladder.

The worktop was for Denzel, a tall, thin Rastafarian, with long fingers and large, white teeth that shone whenever he smiled. He was a train driver on the Tube. He was also a fitness fanatic. Denzel couldn't do anything without also exercising. His flat consisted of two ten-foot rooms and a box room that had a bath in it. It had been converted into a studio flat in the sixties and nothing had been done to it since then. His existing kitchen worktop was rotten beyond repair. I had measured it up and given him a price to replace it over a year ago. 'I need to t'ink about it,' he had said in his slow, deep Caribbean drawl. Denzel pondered my proposition for almost exactly a year. Then, out of the blue, he called me. Today was the only day he could do because he'd been drafted in to do a lot of extra shifts on the District Line. So, I couldn't delay it.

When I got back, the worktop was leaning up against the front of the house. Ryan was nowhere to be seen. Up in the flat, Denzel was lifting weights and doing squat thrusts in a pair of tight Lycra shorts that left very little to the imagination. Denzel had a huge bird-eating spider, which he kept in a tank on top of his wardrobe. It seemed that while Chris was talking at him, Denzel had lifted the lid to feed the spider and it jumped out and wedged itself behind the hot-water tank.

'What's going on?' I said, running up the stairs. 'There's hot water pissing out the window!' Chris was draining the water out of the hot-water tank, so he could move it to catch the spider.

'The hose pipe wasn't long enough to go down the stairs,' said Chris.

'You could scald someone! You're pouring hot water out of a third-floor window!'

'There's a hole behind the tank. It could get stuck under the floorboards,' said Denzel, lunging forward, lifting his arms mid-squat thrust.

'Where's Ryan?'

'He's gone to buy some fags.'

'This is not my problem. I need to get this worktop in and that's it,' I said, taking some wire wool out of my tool-box and shoving it into the hole behind the tank. Chris turned off the drain valve and I called Ryan. I called him six times. Each time there was no answer. When he eventually turned up, he was completely rat-arsed.

'Where the fuck have you been?' I said, as he weaved his way towards the front of the house, then tripped over his crutches.

'I just thought I'd 'ave a wee dram of Jameson's to sober up,' he said, slurring his words.

'For fuck's sake, Ryan! It's eleven o'clock in the bloody morning!' I said, storming off. When I calmed down, I called Big Pete to see if he could help me push the worktop up the ladder. Chris and I both suffered from vertigo and there was no way Ryan could climb a ladder in the state he was in. As luck would have it, Big Pete wasn't far away, so I went to pick him up. I didn't know at the time that Big Pete was scared of only two things: heights and spiders. I positioned the ladder at the front of the house.

'There's no way I'm going up there with that,' he said, leaning the worktop up against the ladder. Chris stayed upstairs and waited by the window. Big Pete stayed downstairs and footed the ladder because the spider was still missing. I told Ryan to go home as he was no good for anything, so it was left to me to slide the worktop up the ladder. As I climbed, I pushed the extremely heavy worktop up with my right hand. When I was halfway up, Denzel appeared, carrying some dumb-bells. 'I got to go out. I left a set of keys on the side,' he said, walking down the road doing bicep curls, then stopping to do a star jump. The wind was picking up and it was starting to drizzle. The ladder was greasy and wobbled under the combined weight of the worktop and me. I was getting very anxious. By the time I was three quarters of the way up, I felt the fear. I knew there was no way back. I had to keep going. As I kept climbing higher, the ladder began to buckle.

'Just a bit further. One more push,' said Chris, leaning out of the window and trying to reach it. I gave it one last push, but it veered off sideways. Chris leant forward to try to catch it and almost fell out of the window. Big Pete jumped off the bottom of the ladder, fearing it was about to fall. I let go of the ladder, grabbed the worktop with my left hand, and used all my strength to pull it straight. I was twenty feet up. The wind was whistling around me and I wasn't holding on. It was a miracle I didn't fall. I imagined Jo at my funeral – still furious that our daughter had missed her cranial appointment and that our son didn't get to go to his chess tournament. When Chris grabbed the worktop, I almost fainted. I held onto the ladder with both hands as Chris tried to pull it up.

'I can't do it,' he said softly under his breath, labouring under the weight, 'I can't tip it up and pull it up on my own.'

'Pete, go and help him,' I screamed, trying to push it with my right hand. Big Pete ran up those stairs like a charging rhinoceros. But when he got to the top, the door was locked. 'You're going to have to hold it. The door's locked. He can't get in. I need to open the door for him,' shouted Chris. I could feel the lactic acid building up in my biceps. I braced myself, grabbed the ladder with both hands and rested the worktop on the inside of my elbows. 'Okay, let go,' I shouted. I felt the full weight rest on the crack of my arms. It cut off the blood supply to my hands. The cut on my knuckle opened up and blood started running down my arm, staining my T-shirt. I knew if I let go, the worktop would crash down and take me with it. I locked my legs and waited, as my hands slowly started to turn blue. With no one footing the ladder, I was terrified it was going to slip. It seemed like an age before Chris and Big Pete appeared at the window.

'It won't fit,' said Chris leaning out of the window with his trusty tape measure. 'I've measured it. The room's too short.'

'I don't care, take it before I fucking fall!' I screamed.

At that moment, Denzel walked in and dropped the dumb-bells down on the floor next to the hot-water tank. The spider raced across the room. Big Pete let go of the worktop and bolted for the bedroom. Chris grabbed it with both hands just as I was about to let go, while Denzel chased his pet with a dustpan and brush.

Thirty seconds later, Denzel walked into the bedroom with the spider trapped in the dustpan. Big Pete was quivering in the corner.

'Take it easy man, it's blocked by the bristles of the brush,' he said, smiling, as he deposited the absconded arachnid back into its tank.

'I'm terrified of tarantulas,' said Big Pete, walking quickly past the wardrobe to help Chris tilt the worktop and pull it in through the window.

Big Pete and Chris hoisted it in far enough to allow it to rest on the sill. It took me a few minutes to build up the courage to climb down the ladder. When I made it to the bottom, I completely collapsed. Chris was right. The room was too short for the length of the worktop. So, we had to cut it with part of it hanging out of the window. We finally finished it at 2.45 p.m. I left Chris and Big Pete to tidy up and drove like a madman to pick up my daughter. She was sitting in the foyer of her nursery with her red woollen Inca hat on and her pink waterproof coat buttoned up to her chin.

'Thank you so much for getting her ready,' I said, bursting in, covered in blood. I looked as if I'd been in a car crash.

'She's refused to take them off all day,' said her key worker, looking at me sideways. 'She kept saying, "I'm not staying. My dad's coming to get me".' I thanked her profusely, picked up my daughter and walked calmly out of the nursery. When I got to the front gate, I started sprinting. Her hat went flying. Her wellies fell off. It was a disaster. I ran twenty feet, then had to stop, turn around and spend the next two minutes picking up everything she'd dropped. We finally got to her cranial appointment fifteen minutes late. It was clear I was not in a good way, but the therapist didn't care. I had to pay her anyway. Fortunately, she agreed to do a quick ten-minute session and promised not to tell Jo. Biblical redemption, my arse! What a load of bollocks! I couldn't believe Jo had fallen for this crap. When the therapist had finished, she started telling me all about crystal therapy. 'I really feel your daughter would benefit from their unique healing qualities,' she said.

I had to go. I was supposed to have picked Oli up – five minutes ago. So, as soon as she had finished telling me about how crystals would prevent bad energy and transform the body's aura, I signed my daughter up to God knows what, put her on my shoulders and ran as fast as I could to my son's primary school. He was standing in the playground, all alone.

'I'm so sorry,' I said, letting go of my daughter's legs and bending down to give him a hug. She tipped backwards, fell off my back and landed on her head.

'No,' I screamed, picking her up, dusting her down and checking for any broken bones. She was fine, just a bit dazed – her Inca hat had cushioned the blow. But so much for the fifty quid I had just spent on cranial therapy. I put her back on my shoulders, grabbed my son's schoolbag and marched them both home. Now, all I had to do was get him to Harrow to play chess. There was no time to change, so I bundled them both into the car and drove straight there.

When we arrived, it was clear that Oli was way out of his depth. He knew only two opening moves. The other kids had been studying chess since before they were born. Their parents had whispered chess moves to them while they were still in the womb. The hall had been specially set up for the occasion. Small tables stood in rows. Chess boards had been set up. Everyone was taking it extremely seriously. Officials were walking up and down the aisles.

Parents weren't allowed into the hall, for fear that they might coach their children, or possibly even attack their opponents. So all the mums and dads had to sit outside in the hallway. Most of them were anxiously playing chess, trying to distract themselves from the palpable tension that had engulfed the entire building. Children came out crying. One boy locked himself in the loo. 'It doesn't matter, son, you weren't to know,' I heard one dad say, trying to console his distraught son. It was a middle-class war zone. Boys were walking the corridors in a state of chess-induced shell shock. I settled down and decided to teach my daughter how to play chess.

'No, I want to put it there,' she said, moving her pawn sideways.

'No, you can't do that.'

'I'm putting it there,' she said, forcefully.

'Okay, ' I conceded. 'Who needs rules.'

There was a short, squat man sitting next to me, who kept tutting at me. He clearly disapproved of my daughter's refusal to follow the rules. Then his son came out of the hall, wearing dark-green corduroy trousers and a sports jacket – he looked like he taught Classics at Cambridge. I thought at any moment he was going to start smoking a pipe, despite being only eight.

'I'm so sorry, Dad,' he said, as a tear rolled down his cheek.

'What happened?' said the man, clearly shocked to see him back so soon.

'I lost. I'm so sorry.'

'What? How?' he said, leaping to his feet.

'I don't know. He took my queen.'

'No! Not your queen!' he said, holding his head in his hands. 'Show me!' he said, quickly setting up a chessboard. I honestly thought he was taking the piss, but he wasn't; he was deadly serious.

In contrast, Oli played five games of chess that afternoon and lost every single one in less than five minutes. They all knew how to combat his opening moves. But he didn't care. He came bounding out, laughing at how crap he'd been. Then he did a quick pirouette, lifted his leg up to his ear and said, 'I lost that one, too. Can we go to McDonald's now?'

I knew then that he was never going to be a chess champion, and McDonald's seemed like an excellent idea, so I bundled them into the car and headed for Miriam's house in Hampstead. As we were leaving, the man who'd heard me humouring my daughter turned to me and said, 'She'll never be any good if you don't teach her the rules.' That tipped me over the edge.

'We've just been to McDonald's!' said my son, as soon as we arrived at Miriam's house. Jo glared at me as she quartered the sandwiches. Miriam didn't approve of fast food.

'Dad let me have a bacon double cheeseburger.'

He couldn't really have said anything worse. Char siu and tandoori king prawns were fine, but bacon was strictly off limits.

'You can't come in here looking like that, I've got people coming,' said Miriam, looking at me disapprovingly.

'You took them looking like that!' said Jo in horror, pointing at my filthy plumbing trousers, my blood-stained T-shirt and my reversed baseball cap.

'For God's sake, get away from the house, someone might see you. I'll bring them home after the meeting,' said Miriam.

I felt utterly exhausted. So I left them, and drove home.

Two-and-a-half hours later, Jo got home and put the kids straight to bed. I was asleep on the sofa. 'So you were late getting her to her cranial appointment, you signed her up for some crystal sessions, dropped her on her head, told Oli that all chess players have freaky foreheads, laughed at a man trying to console his son and then told him to fuck off?' she said, hitting me over the head with a cushion.

'I can explain,' I said, holding up my hands to defend myself.

'*Can* you?' she said, retracting the cushion to hit me again.

'No, not really …'

I realised then that my life really was like a game of chess. No matter how much I tried to plan ahead, I always ended up reacting to what was in front of me, and it didn't take much for everything to fall apart. 'It's like chess,' I said, trying to stop her from hitting me with the cushion.

'You can't castle your way out of this one,' she said, smiling.

'How was the chavurah?'

'Surprisingly okay. Mum doesn't mean it. She can't help it. She was indoctrinated as a child. Come on, let's go to bed,' she said, leaning forward to kiss me – moving her queen into position.

'Checkmate!' I whispered as we turned off the lights.

5

The Judge and the Dentist

I was installing a bathroom for my dentist in Dartmouth Park when I began to realise that I was no longer in charge of my own life. I can't remember exactly when it happened. It wasn't like there was a Eureka moment when I suddenly woke up and smelled the coffee. It was a gradual process. The more middle-aged women I worked for, the more I realised that they were the ones who were really calling the shots. They allowed their husbands to think they were making the decisions, but, behind the scenes, it was the women pulling the strings. When it came to making the big, life-changing decisions, they were the ones in charge. Should they have kids? When should they have kids? Where should they live? What particular house or flat should they live in? How much should they spend on it? How should it look? Where should their kids go to school? How involved should they be in their schooling? How often should the kids see her mother? The list went on and on. And the more I saw it, the more I realised that this is what had happened to me. Jo was in charge. She made all the decisions, not me. While I was working for my dentist, she told me the old Jewish joke about the boy who ran home to tell his mother that he'd just been given a part in the new school play.

'That's wonderful, darling! What part did you get?' said the mother.

'I got the part of the husband!' he said, proudly.

'That's marvellous, but couldn't they give you a speaking part?'

Estate agents don't sell houses to husbands, they sell them to their wives, and my business was exactly the same. Sell it to the wife, she would work on her husband and eventually get him to agree. It was a winning formula and, as my experience expanded, I became an expert at winning over difficult, demanding, wealthy women who wanted something new, but didn't know what. The best way to get to these women was through other women just like them. Women communicate. They talk to each other. They share experiences and, if you get it right, they recommend you. And when they do that, you've pretty much got the job before you even walk in the door. It's as simple as that.

I have, of course, come across exceptions: men who have suffered some kind of trauma in childhood and consequently exercise excessive control over their wives. These men were also often extremely wealthy, were nearly always control freaks, and generally didn't have happy marriages. As a result, they were very risky to work for. This was partly because working for control freaks is extremely draining, but also because building a new bathroom can easily become illustrative of wider problems in their relationship and, before you know it, you get drawn in to their marital conflicts, which, more often than not, cannot be fixed with a spanner.

My dentist was a very brusque woman, with short black hair and a smile that lingered slightly too long. Before my first visit to see her, Jo had told her that I hadn't been to the dentist since I was a child.

'What?' the dentist screamed.

'That's the most ridiculous thing I've ever heard! Sit down immediately and let's have a good look at you!'

I could tell, despite her rather aggressive manner, that she was fundamentally a very kind woman and, over the course of the next ten years, I grew to be really quite fond of her. She had been Jo's dentist since she was a little girl and she still sometimes gave Jo stickers for good flossing, which I thought was slightly strange since Jo was almost thirty.

Shortly after my first visit, Jo told her that I was retraining to become a plumber, so I could earn some money while I was writing my first novel. She liked that. It appealed to her artistic side. Unfortunately, from then on she always asked me if my book had been published yet.

'Why not?' she would exclaim, powering up her drill and encouraging me to open wide.

'You've not been flossing! No sticker for you!' she would say, poking around in my mouth, tutting underneath her breath. I had come to dread her questioning almost as much as her drill.

★ ★ ★ ★

After about a year of appointments, and after a particularly painful root canal, she asked me if I would rebuild her bathroom. I went to see her and gave her a price. Several days later, she agreed, and I started the following week. On my first day, I arrived at 7.30 a.m. as I had said I would. She opened the door immediately, wearing a long dressing gown covered in daisies. She asked me if I'd like a cup of tea.

'Yes, please, that would be wonderful,' I replied.

'How do you take it?'

'Milk, with two sugars.'

'Not in this house you don't! No wonder you've got so many fillings!'

'In which case, I'll just have a black coffee,' I replied.

'That's better. Anyway, I only have soya milk. As it happens, I'm meeting a friend this morning. We walk our dogs together up on Hampstead Heath. She also wants a new bathroom. I'll put in a good word for you. Her parents were both writers. Her husband's a bit of a character. I personally don't find him that difficult, but I know some people do; he's a judge. Doesn't suffer fools gladly, but don't worry about him, it's Vicky who calls the shots.'

At around three o'clock that afternoon, her bathroom door suddenly swung open and in marched a big bald man with wide whiskers and a huge Lord Kitchener moustache that was waxed into two points. His hands were the size of dinner plates and his chin almost completely disappeared into the cravat he had around his neck.

'I understand you build bathrooms,' he said, with military enunciation and an extremely posh public-school accent.

'Yes,' I said, somewhat taken aback.

'Good,' he said, looking me up and down. 'Come and see me at 5.30 this afternoon. I live just up the road. Here's my address,' he said, thrusting a piece of paper into my hand, turning round and marching back out of the bathroom, slamming the door behind him.

To be honest, I wasn't quite sure what to make of it. There was a part of me that was slightly intrigued, yet I also wasn't sure I wanted to work for a man like that. Nevertheless, at

5.30 p.m. I found myself driving up the road and parking outside his house at the bottom of Highgate, and what a house it was. Originally built in 1660, it was one of the great old houses of London. I walked slowly up the path that led to the front door and hesitated slightly before I knocked. No sooner had I taken my hand off the knocker, than the door opened.

'Good, I can't abide people who are late. Come with me,' he said, marching briskly through the living room and then up two flights of stairs to the top of the house.

'This is it. What we want is a new bathroom, and to change that God-awful radiator. As you can see, it's all original. Hasn't been touched since the turn of the century. I've had a few people look at it over the years, but they've always wanted too much money. I understand you are different. I'm told you write. Good. My parents-in-law were both writers. My wife likes the idea of helping a struggling writer. Are you struggling?'

'Yes, I suppose I am.'

'Good. I don't want to spend any more than £5,000. That's it! Take it or leave it. Do you want the job?'

'Okay,' I said, hesitating slightly. 'It will depend on what fixtures and fittings you want. I can't say that I will do it for £5,000 if you want £3,000-worth of sanitary ware.'

'I'll buy all the gubbins. I just need you to install them.'

'I can probably buy it for less than you can, but that's up to you.'

'Okay, £5,000 plus whatever the stuff costs. Do we have a deal?'

'I don't know.'

'What do you mean, you don't know? You either want the job or you don't! What is there to think about?'

'I really need to go away and work it out. This is a very old house. I suspect you've got lots of old lead pipes hidden in the walls. Give me a few days and I will get back to you.'

'Get back to me! For God's sake. *Really*?'

'Yes, I need to work it out, whether I can do it for that or not.'

'Leave him alone, Peter,' came a gentle voice from the bottom of the stairs, 'It's perfectly reasonable for him to need to go away and work it out. Stop bullying him!'

Thirty seconds later, Vicky, his wife, appeared at the top of the stairs. 'I'm so sorry, he doesn't mean it. It comes from having too much power at work. Why don't you talk to me about it and then I'll talk to Peter.' Vicky had the class and effortless charm of a woman who'd never had to struggle. She wafted into a room. She was eloquent, artistic and very amusing. She had clearly been very beautiful as a young woman. She was still beautiful, even approaching seventy. She had an easy confidence that came from having had men fawn over her. I knew almost immediately that we would get on and, by the time I left, I was fairly certain I'd already got the job. But I still had to get past Peter. So, a couple of days later, I did what Vicky had told me to do. I called him up and told him that I was very sorry, I had priced it up and, owing to a number of factors, primarily due to the age of the property, I wasn't going to be able to do it for the amount he wanted to pay. The least I could do it for would be £6,000 plus the cost of the sanitary ware. I added that I completely understood that that was more than his budget and I was sure he would be able to find someone else who would do the job for what he wanted to pay, and I wished him the best of luck. He didn't say a thing. He just waited for me to finish, then said, 'I see,' and slammed the phone down. I thought that was it and I would never hear from him again, but, several days later, my phone rang. 'Do you want the bloody job or not?' said Peter, angrily.

'Yes, but only if you're prepared to pay me what I've quoted.'

'All right. Vicky wants you to do it. When can you start?'

'In two weeks time?'

'Two weeks!'

'Yes, I'm busy until then.'

'Fine. What date?'

'Monday the 23rd."

'Good. Be here at 7.30 and don't be late!'

'Tell him to park on the drive,' I heard Vicky say in the background. 'Darling, you can put your car out on the road, otherwise I'll have to be constantly giving him parking permits.'

'I'll tell him that when he gets here. I've told him he's got the job. Isn't that enough?' And, with that, he slammed the phone down.

On my first day, Vicky answered the door, looking very glamorous.

'I'm so pleased you came to an agreement with Peter,' she said, as if she'd had nothing to do with it. 'I'm an artist and I've got a show in a month, so you'll have to excuse the mess,' she said, showing me past a line of unframed paintings, then down the stairs into the kitchen. Peter was sitting at the kitchen table eating his smoked mackerel. 'Sorry about the smell. Peter had a mild heart attack a few months ago, so now he's only eating oily fish,' she said, looking over at him as he immersed himself in his newspaper. 'Can I get you a cup of tea?'

'He's not here to drink tea,' said Peter, without looking up from his paper.

'Ignore him, he's always grumpy in the morning.'

'I have to be in court this morning, so if you have any questions, you'd better ask me now,' he said, still not looking up from his paper. 'Did she show you where to park? Kicked off my own driveway by the bloody plumber!'

'As I said, just ignore him. He's got a particularly difficult case going on at the moment.'

'I understand. Do you know where the stopcock is by any chance?'

Peter growled, 'In the basement. But don't turn it off until I've left. I want to brush my teeth. Can't go into court smelling like Grimsby fish market. Anything else?' he shouted, still not looking up from his paper.

'Do you have any tanks up in the loft?'

'How the hell do I know? Go and have a look!'

'At some point, I'm going to need some money, just to cover all my fixtures and fittings.'

'For God's sake!' he shouted. 'All right, come with me.' He stood up and marched out of the kitchen. He led me up one flight of stairs, past more paintings, waiting to be framed, and into his study.

'Do not, under any circumstances, interrupt me when I am in here! How much do you want?'

'A thousand pounds should cover it. As per my estimate. Then if you can pay me at the end of each week, for the work that I've done that week, I'd be very grateful.'

He opened his desk, took out a Coutts cheque-book and wrote me a cheque.

'Here's five thousand pounds. Don't ask me for any more until it's done!'

Half an hour later, after I had brought all my tools in, laid out some dust sheets to protect the carpets and cleared out the bathroom, Peter left and I made my way back downstairs. Vicky was standing at the end of the kitchen, looking at a painting she had just completed. 'What do you think?' she said.

'I absolutely love that,' I replied.

'Do you? Yes, it is rather nice, isn't it.'

'How much do you want for it?'

'Two hundred and sixty pounds. It will be framed, of course.'

'I might buy it,' I said.

'Oh, really?'

'Yes, I really like it.'

'I've promised I'll put it in the show.'

'That's fine. You can put it in the show and then I'll buy it. I'll need some time to get it past my wife!'

She laughed. 'Okay,' she said.

'It was a pleasure doing business with you. Now, where's the basement?' I said, walking back out of the kitchen.

'Oh, it's just over here,' said Vicky, showing me a door on the other side of the dining room. The light's on the right-hand side. Mind your head as you go down.'

In the centre of the cellar was an old, disused well, with a bucket and pulley over the top of it. 'That was how they used to get the water for the house,' said Vicky from the top of the stairs. 'Then they'd heat it in the kitchen and take it upstairs. The mains were installed in the mid-1870s, when they built the Underground. This was one of the first houses to have indoor plumbing in the whole of Highgate,' she said, proudly.

'Amazing!' I said, as my heart sank. 'I've so under-estimated this,' I thought to myself as I inspected the enormous lead main, which was the width of my forearm. At the far end of the cellar was an enormous stop valve. It was five times the size of a normal one and clearly hadn't been turned off for at least fifty years. This was by far the most valuable house I had ever worked in. It must have been worth at least £5 or £6 million. You could fit my entire flat into just its front room. It was so old that the beams supporting the floors had twisted and shrunk over the years, which meant that some of the floors sloped so significantly that the pieces of furniture had to be nailed to the floor to stop them sliding around. I pushed and pulled at the valve for ages, before I eventually went to get some grips from my van so I could get more leverage.

When the valve finally gave way, there was a very disturbing rumbling sound and the whole cellar started to shake. I broke into an immediate cold sweat. I quickly turned it back on and, slowly, the shaking began to subside. I waited for my heart rate to return to normal, then, after several minutes, I braved the valve again. Once more, the whole room started to shudder. Quickly, I turned it off, and began to back-track. By now, I really was beginning to panic. How the hell was I going to do the job if I couldn't turn the water off! Then, the shuddering started again. Only this time I hadn't gone anywhere near the stop valve. Maybe I'd broken it. Maybe I'd damaged something underground when I was yanking it. Maybe I should turn the water off outside in the street. Maybe I should call Thames Water and get them to turn the whole road off. Maybe I'm going completely mad! As more and more crazy thoughts kept barrelling through my head, the shuddering began to subside, then it stopped completely. I stood there, pondering what it could be, when it happened again, and again, and again. Then it dawned on me. It had absolutely nothing to do with what I was doing. It was the Northern Line! The well shaft was so close to the tunnels that it was acting as a conduit for the movement of the Tube trains as they accelerated off towards Archway. That must have been why the well dried up when they built the Underground, which was why the house was put on the mains.

The following morning, I told Peter what had happened and he roared with laughter as he carefully cooked his kippers. 'I've brought someone with me today to help me take the bath out. He's my wife's godson. He's a student.'

'A student! What's he studying?'

'Astrophysics.'

'Astrophysics! Where?'

'Imperial.'

'Good. Let me know when the astrophysicist has taken my bloody bath out!' he said, tucking into his toast.

Several hours later, I realised there was absolutely no way that we were going to be able to take the old cast-iron bath out in one piece. It weighed almost 200 kilograms. If either of us dropped it while we were carrying it down the stairs, it would probably kill whoever was below, and take out the entire staircase and the floors below. The normal practice in this situation is to smash up the bath unless it's needed for some reason; since the metal is hard and brittle it just needs attacking with a heavy hammer. I went out and bought two sets of ear defenders and two large sledge-hammers. Then we turned it upside down, waited for Vicky to go out and took turns to hit it as hard as we could until, finally, it cracked and broke into pieces. It took us almost two hours to smash it up. Later that week, several people wrote in to the *Ham & High*, the local newspaper for Hampstead and Highgate, complaining about a very loud bell, which had been rung incessantly for several hours on Tuesday morning.

The day after the letters were published, Peter wasn't very happy and, as soon as I arrived, he called me into his study. 'There have been several complaints about noise!' he said. 'I have received reports of a large bell being rung on Tuesday morning, causing a disturbance to the peace! Do you know anything about this?' I explained the situation and, again, he roared with laughter. 'Serves them bloody well right. It's probably the same bastards who complained about the noise from the Kenwood concerts. Ridiculous! Those concerts have been going on for years. If they have a problem with them, they shouldn't have bought a bloody house near the Heath. What do they expect? I should go round to every house and explain that my plumber is going to have to smash up an old bath in order to get it safely out of my house? Utter nonsense! Anyway, I have been looking through all the bathroom brochures you gave Vicky and I can't find a decent bidet in any of them.'

'Yes, not many people have bidets these days.'

'Well, I like a good bidet and, more importantly, so does my wife! I want an original French bidet with brass taps! Why is it so hard to get brass taps? All taps when I was growing up used to be brass. I can't stand these modern chrome ones, and the gold ones are all just so tacky! I want antique brass taps. Is that really too much to ask?'

The next day, I went straight to my plumbing merchant to order all the sanitary ware.

'Where's Ryan?' said John, seeing the student sitting in the passenger seat of my van.

'He's gone AWOL. Went on a bender for Paddy's Day and I haven't seen him since!'

'That was over a week ago.'

'Yes, I know. Fuck knows where he is.'

'What are you after?'

'A metre of four-inch pipe, two four-inch rubber Fernco fittings to slide over four-inch cast iron and a strap-on boss.'

'Missus asserting her authority again?'

I laughed, but carried on.

'A double-ended Bette bath with two magnetic pillows.'

'Ooh, Betty,' he said, imitating Frank Spencer in the TV comedy *Some Mothers Do 'Ave 'Em*.

'A set of Stuart Turner Edwardian brass bath taps, and the same for the basin.'

'Nice! This one's got money! Which style?'

'These,' I said, leaning forward to show him a picture on my phone.

'Christ, he's really got money to burn.'

'You've no idea. He's a judge. Scary as you like, but absolutely minted. The house is like something out of Harry Potter.'

'You'd better not fuck it up or you'll find yourself in Pentonville.'

'Ding-dong, you're not wrong. And the scariest part is he's already paid me for most of it.'

'Really?'

'Yep, he's that confident that he can get me banged up if he's not happy. Oh, and – you're going to love this – he wants an old, reconditioned, hand-painted French bidet that shoots water straight up your arse.'

'Really?'

'Honest to God.'

'I bet he does.'

'And he wants it with brass taps!'

'Do you want a tub of K-Y Jelly and a gimp mask to go with that?'

'No, I'm sure he's probably already got that.'

'Anything else?'

'No, that'll do.'

'I'll have to source the bidet. Give me a couple of days.'

'No, here you go,' I said, leaning forward to show him a picture on my phone. 'It's a company working out of a cowshed down in Kent. Crazily expensive, but there you are. I'll send you the link.' John pulled it up on his screen and read out the strapline in his best posh accent: 'A reconditioned, hand-painted, French bidet (circa 1920) with a nozzle set into the base of the pan that shoots mixed warm water upwards to clean those hard-to-reach places.' He burst out laughing. 'You've got to be kidding me?'

'I know.'

'What's wrong with doing a handstand in the shower?'

'I know. These rich folks always have to be different.'

The next day, I lifted the floor, and the true horror of what I was facing became abundantly clear. The first problem was that all the pipes feeding the 'God-awful' radiator were in cast iron. This meant that to take the radiator out, I had to unscrew the pipes. However, they had been in place for over a hundred years and had completely seized. On top of this, they weren't fastened down, so every time I tried to turn them, the whole pipe banged against the underside of the floorboards, all the way down the stairs. Eventually, I gave up and cut the cast-iron pipe with a hacksaw. However, cast-iron fittings aren't something I carry, so I had to drive half-way across London to buy a fitting. The next issue was the lead pipes which fed the bath and the toilet. They were so brittle that moving them caused them to split, which meant I basically had to re-pipe the whole room. The third problem was the floor: it sloped sharply from left to right and had a bulge in the middle where a joist had twisted, all of which made it almost impossible to tile. Gradually, I worked through all the issues with Vicky, then, when I was half-way through the job, Peter came upstairs to inspect what I had done.

'I understand you went to Uppingham?' he said, appearing in the doorway.

'Yes, I did.'

'One of my best friends went there.'

'Ah, really? Which house was he in?'

'How the devil should I know? Vicky tells me you studied law at university.'

'Yes, that's right. Law and politics, actually.'

'Did you go to law school?'

'No, I realised quite early on that law wasn't for me.'

'And plumbing is?'

'Well, yes, kind of.'

'What do you mean, "kind of"?'

'I actually did a postgraduate diploma in book publishing after I finished my degree. My idea was to get a job as a book publisher and learn how the business worked and then submit my own manuscript.'

'Good plan. Doesn't explain why you are a plumber though, does it?'

'When I finished my postgrad, my father cut me off and I was forced to get the first job I could.'

'And that was as a plumber?'

'No, not quite. There were several stages in between. I became a plumber when my son was born because I wanted to earn some money while I was writing, and there was a shortage of plumbers at the time.'

'What are you writing?'

'A novel about a man struggling to come to terms with his own childhood while his wife is giving birth to their first child.'

'It sounds autobiographical. Is it?'

'Well, they say you should write about what you know best.'

'Do they?' he said, turning round and walking back towards the top of the stairs.

The next day, I lifted a floorboard outside the bathroom and discovered a small tin wrapped in newspaper. Presuming it predated the current owners, I opened it. Inside were several letters, neatly folded and held together with a piece of string. I slackened the string and took out the first letter.

It started, 'Dearest Vicky, It feels like an age since I last saw you ...'

I quickly closed it and put it back in the tin, then I took it downstairs and gave it to Vicky.

'I found this underneath a floorboard,' I said, handing it to her. 'I haven't read any of them, I just opened the lid and saw that they were addressed to you.'

'Oh my word! I haven't seen that for almost fifty years. I must have hidden them to stop my mother from reading them. They're from Peter. Before we were married. When we were at university together.'

'Is that how you met?'

'Yes. He was such a rebel back then.'

'Really?' I said, somewhat surprised. 'Which university did you go to?'

'Cambridge. He was studying English and I was studying History of Art. He crashed his bike into mine when he was cycling home after a night in The Free Press.'

'That's a pub I assume?'

'Yes.'

'Drunk and in charge of a bicycle? Tut-tut.'

'Yes, he was, but don't tell him I told you! He was so sweet back then. He offered to fix my bike, which he did. He actually had it delivered round to my college a few days later. He'd even put a red bow on it! Inside the basket was a letter asking me to meet him for tea at his favourite tea shop.'

'Was that it?'

'No. Life is never that simple. I was going out with someone else at the time. My father hated him. Rupert. He was far too strait-laced for me. No, we met again when I came back to London. Peter was at law school, training to become a barrister, and Rupert and I had just split up. Daddy wasn't too impressed. He wanted me to marry a pirate and sail the seven seas. Peter was everything that Daddy wasn't. He was trustworthy, reliable, financially stable and he didn't really mind me bossing him around. In fact, I think he quite enjoyed it.'

'So Peter was part of your rebellion?'

'Yes, I suppose he was. Daddy used to say, "For God's sake, get rid of him and find a young buccaneer who'll bring some excitement into your life!" Daddy's idea of excitement was leaving my mum for months on end while he gallivanted round the globe, banging out his latest bestseller. Writers can be very selfish, you know.'

'Yes, I know.'

'And the more successful they are, the worse they become. Remember that. Artists have a tendency to destroy everything they love. They can't help it. I know. I watched it destroy my parents.'

'Is that why you married Peter?'

'Yes, partly. He adored me. He still does. He brought some balance into my life. He's a sweetheart, really. He comes across as a bully, but he isn't really. It's all just an act. He's actually very kind and sensitive underneath. He's been a great father to our daughter, much better than my father was to me. You've just got to know how to penetrate his armour, that's all. Anyway, thank you for finding these; I'll enjoy re-reading them. I might even show them to Peter.'

The next day, Peter arrived home, looking very pleased with himself. The case had clearly come to a conclusion. I heard the slight whirr of an old gramophone, followed by the crackle of the vinyl as the needle slipped into its groove. Then, the sound of Chopin's first piano concerto rose up the staircase, filling the house with an air of structured calm. The sun was shining through the large leaded window at the top of the stairs; I stopped what I was doing to take in the atmosphere. Suddenly, Peter appeared, silhouetted against the brilliance of the sunbeams behind him. He smelt of whisky and was feasting on a Tupperware of whelks. 'Are you busy?' he asked, almost gently. 'I have something I want to talk to you about.' I rolled out from underneath the bath and put down my pipe wrench. 'How can I help?' I said, standing up.

'Vicky tells me you found my letters.'

'Yes, I did, but don't worry, I didn't read them.'

'So she tells me. Weren't you curious?'

'No, not really. I opened the box and took out the first letter, but as soon as I realised they were addressed to Vicky I folded it up and went downstairs to give the box to her.'

'Good. Vicky tells me you live in Crouch End?'

'Yes, that's right.'

'I understand that Crouch End is becoming quite popular now.'

'Yes, I suppose it is.'

'In my day it was full of bedsits with paraffin heaters.'

'It's not like that now.'

'So I understand. This leads me to my question. As well as being a judge, I am also a landlord and over the years I have acquired a number of shops in various parts of London. They are my pension.'

'Why shops?' I enquired.

'Because the yield is higher than residential property.'

'As a matter of interest, what is their average yield?'

'Six or seven per cent per annum.'

'That's good, much better than in residential letting.'

'Yes, I know. That's why I do it. Anyway, a property in Crouch End is for sale. I may be interested in purchasing it, but, before I do, I thought I would ask you what you think about it since you live there and I understand you have done for many years. It's not far from The King's Head at the bottom of Coleridge Road. It has a "For Sale" sign outside. Go and have a look and let me know if you think it would be a good investment.'

Several days later, I finished the bathroom and invited Vicky and Peter to come up and have a look. Vicky was at the bottom of the garden feeding the fish in her ornamental pond. The branches of a couple of large weeping willows were swaying in the breeze and some delicate antique bronze ducks were sunning themselves on the edge of the lawn. Peter was listening to Debussy in his study when Vicky knocked on the door. 'Enter,' he barked, sliding his signet ring on and off the little finger of his left hand.

'Nick has finished the bathroom and he'd like you to come and take a look at it,' she said.

'It's about time,' he growled, standing up and marching up the stairs. I showed them how everything worked, and Vicky absolutely loved it. Peter said nothing until I ran out of things to say. There was a rather awkward silence and then he said, 'I suppose you want some money,' walking out of the room. 'You had better follow me.' Settling up at the end of a job is always slightly unnerving and this time was no exception. Fortunately, I had come prepared. I'd put together a spreadsheet of all my expenditure. I had broken my labour charge down by the day, so he could see exactly how I'd calculated the final figure, in line with my original estimate. Peter sat down at his desk and leant forward to turn the Debussy down. 'Right, so how much do you want?' he said, unbuckling his watch strap and slowly winding his watch in front of me. I handed him the spreadsheet and he glanced at it. 'Never mind all that. How much do you want?'

'Well, I did it in slightly less time than I thought, but I had to buy a lot of extra, unusual fittings to make everything fit.'

'Spit it out, man, for God's sake. I'm losing the will to live!' he said, putting his watch back on his wrist.

'In total, it comes to £6,260.'

'What!' he bellowed.

'But, as you know, you've already paid me £5,000, so that leaves £1,260.'

'How on earth did you come up with that?'

'If you look at my spreadsheet …'

'I don't want to look at your creative accounting. Tell me why I should pay you another £1,200.'

'Because that's what you agreed to before I started the job.'

'I did no such thing!'

'Well, as it happens, I was talking to Vicky this morning about one of the paintings she is exhibiting at her show and she has agreed to sell it to me for £260, so if you make the cheque out for £1,000, which is exactly what my initial estimate was, then I'll take the painting and we can each go our separate ways.'

'Which painting is it?'

'It's the silhouette of a woman walking up some stairs.'

'Not the one at the bottom of the stairs in the gold frame?'

'Yes, that's the one.'

'I've promised that one to a friend of mine. I've told him he can have it. So sorry, it's not for sale.'

'Oh, what a shame,' I said, disappointed. 'I'd really fallen in love with that painting.'

'How much did you say you wanted?'

'Well, if I can't have the painting, if you can make it out for the full outstanding amount then that would be great.'

'You were right about that shop, by the way.'

'Oh good. It's in a funny location. It's not on the main drag. Whoever rents it might regret it.'

'Yes, I can see that,' he said, passing me another Coutts cheque.

'Thank you,' I said, taking the cheque.

'I'm sorry about the painting,' he said, standing up to shake my hand.

When I got to the bottom of the stairs, Vicky thanked me profusely for all my hard work, as the sound of Debussy's '*Clair de lune*' drifted out of the windows of Peter's study. 'I look forward to reading your novel. Did you tell Peter about the painting?' she asked, putting her arm around me.

'Yes, I did, but unfortunately he's promised it to someone else.'

'Yes, I know, but I bet it threw him off guard?' she said, winking at me. 'Did he pay you what you wanted?'

'Yes, he did.'

'Good. That's because he felt guilty about the painting. Otherwise, he'd have made you account for everything. I'm sorry about the picture, but please do come to the exhibition.'

'Thank you. I will.'

'And remember what I said about writers. When you're successful, remember what I said.'

'Is that why I got the job?'

'Yes, partly, but I understand your wife is lovely. She sent my friend, your dentist, the most lovely letter when her husband died.'

'That's right, she did.'

'That's really why you got the job, not because you're a writer. As you've no doubt gathered, I have a complicated relationship with creatives. But good women need to stick together,' she said, shaking my hand and carefully closing the door behind me.

'Thank God for that,' I heard Peter say, as I saw him looking out of the window of his study, as I got to the end of path. 'I can have my bloody parking space back,' were the last words I heard him say as I bundled my tools into the back of my van.

★ ★ ★ ★

Two weeks later, on the day of Vicky's exhibition, I happened to have a dental appointment. 'I'm loving my new shower,' said my dentist, as I sat down in her chair and leant back. 'And Vicky's raving about her new bathroom. She told me how you dealt with Peter,' she said, sticking her finger into my mouth. 'That was a complete stroke of genius! In all the years I've known them, I don't think anyone has managed to get Peter to settle up properly at the end of a job. He always overpays at the beginning and then negotiates at the end. It drives Vicky mad. He had a decorator in tears last year.'

'Well, I did have some help,' I mumbled, as she poked around inside my mouth.

'I know. She's wonderful, isn't she? I told you she calls the shots. But never mind that ... Bite down on this. I'm going to have to take some X-rays,' she said, moving the X-ray machine next to my right cheek, then leaving the room. Several seconds later she came back into the room. 'Vicky told me you're still taking sugar in your tea!' she said, looking at me intently. 'No wonder you need two more fillings! There's no sticker for you this week,' she said, sitting down behind me. 'Fortunately, they aren't that deep, so I think I can do it without any anaesthetic. Serves you right,' she said, putting on her glasses and powering up her drill. 'Just relax and open wide,' she said, placing the sucker into the side of my mouth.' I closed my eyes and grabbed the arms of the chair just as she lowered the drill. 'This might tickle a bit,' she said, smiling under her breath. 'Since I've given you two jobs, I was wondering if you could come and have a look at my downstairs toilet? I don't want any favours, but maybe we could do an exchange? I won't charge you for your fillings, and you could come and fix my toilet. What do you say?' I nodded. 'Good. Well, that's settled then. And no more sugar in your tea. I'll find out!'

6

Justice on Tap

Over the years, I've been asked if I can replace windows, recycle furniture, get rid of vermin, strip floorboards, build water features, assemble wardrobes, put up pictures, stick mirrors to walls, install decking, put up shelves and even sell cars. I've even got a little black book full of things I've done to keep my clients happy. Some people seem to think that because I can do something they can't, this means I can do anything. 'While you're here, would you mind just doing this. It shouldn't take you too long,' is the classic phrase. They then invariably show me something that's got absolutely nothing to do with plumbing and is clearly going to take me hours, if not days, to sort out. For example, one person asked me if I could hotwire the lead on his roof to the electricity supply, to stop thieves from stealing it. Another asked me if I would by-pass his gas meter so he wouldn't have to pay for it. When I refused, he asked me if I could plumb his radiators to his neighbour's heating system. I obviously didn't do any of these things, but sometimes doing the right thing means you have to bend the rules; and knowing where to draw the line isn't always easy. That was the dilemma when I was working for Clarissa.

There was a vulnerability to Clarissa that made me really want to help her, much more than any of the other mothers at my children's primary school. I really liked her and, in hindsight, I probably let that cloud my judgement. Clarissa had a kind of easy-going confidence, eyes that loved to laugh and a smile that quickly turned into a grin. It was as if her life was a beautiful landscape, painted in broad brush-strokes, best viewed from afar. She didn't bother with all the awkward little details. She was better than that. She was an artist. A real class act. Of course she could also be extremely neurotic and at times really quite paranoid, but beneath it all there was always an understated grandeur to her. She had grown up in very privileged surroundings, but she wasn't at all judgemental and was always very considerate of everyone else's feelings.

In many ways she was an absolute joy to work for and yet, in others, she was a nightmare. She brought me tea and toast every morning. She even cooked me lunch. She would sit down next to me while I was working and ask me loads of questions about what was happening in my life; it really felt as if she was genuinely interested in what I had to say. She had that wonderful gift of being able to make people feel special. As a plumber, that was an extremely rare thing to encounter. Most people just wanted me in and out and couldn't care less who I was. As far as they were concerned, I was just a toilet un-blocker. But not Clarissa. She saw past all that. She saw me for who I was. She was, and still is, a really good person, but good things don't always happen to good people, no matter how hard you try to help them.

Clarissa was the daughter of a famous filmmaker, who, in turn, was the son of another famous filmmaker, who had fled Italy for the UK just before the Second World War. Her father had worked with Fellini. You could see that Clarissa was creative; she looked a bit like a mad scientist. She was slightly scatty, very disorganised, always running late and yet she was also incredibly intelligent and extremely perceptive. She'd read chemistry at Cambridge before she joined the family business. We met because our youngest children were in the same class at primary school. I was waiting in the playground, looking at my first iPhone (that's how long ago it was), trying to avoid making eye contact with any of the mothers, when Clarissa raced into the playground carrying a case full of scripts, a latte and bag full of bagels. Her hair was typically tousled, she was wearing black Lycra running leggings and a very smart blouse; she glistened slightly with perspiration. She looked like she had just left a very important business meeting and then run a marathon. 'I made it!' she said, gasping for breath.

'Yes,' I said.

'They haven't come out yet?'

'No. They're all still sitting on the rug, listening to a story.'

'Thank God for that. I didn't think I was going to make it. I can't bear the thought of her waiting in an empty playground, while all the other children go home. It's the kind of thing that scars them for life! Anyway, I'm here now. There was just such a long queue at the bakers. I promised her we'd have bagel toast for tea. They're her absolute favourite. Do you want one?' she said, offering me the bag.

'No. I'm fine, thanks. You look like you've been running.'

'Oh this? Yes, I've just come from an exercise class. We run up and down the hill at Ally Pally. Me and twelve other middle-aged women in Lycra. It's not a pretty sight.'

'And in such a nice blouse?'

'Thank you. No, I wore this for a meeting earlier. I realised I was going to be short of time, so I put my running clothes on underneath. I didn't run in it. I've got a Lycra running vest on. Look,' she said, lifting the edge of her blouse. 'I just put this on because I didn't want to carry it.'

'If you're running late and ever need someone to pick Tabby up, I'd be happy to do it.'

'Oh, that's so kind of you, but don't worry, I'm always running late. You'd be picking her up every day. I don't understand how everyone does it. It's just beyond me. Anyway, it's very kind of you, but my mum and dad don't live far away.'

'I've seen them picking her up.'

'Yes, they do it quite a lot. I'm very lucky.'

'Well, it sounds like you've got it covered,' I said, as the classroom door swung open and the kids came cascading out.

The next day, when I got to the playground, my daughter was playing chase with Tabby, while her grandma was trying to catch her. 'Can I help?' I said, grabbing my daughter as she raced past me.

'Dad! I was winning. She would never have caught me. She's "it"!'

'I dare say she is, but it's time to go home now. Are you Clarissa's mum by any chance?' I asked the older lady.

'Yes, I am. Thank you so much for catching them, I don't think I would ever have managed it. They're just so fast.'

'I know,' I said, throwing my daughter's schoolbag over my shoulder. 'Clarissa told me you live nearby.'

'Yes, not far, just by Golders Hill Park.'

'That's handy. She said that you're always on hand to help out.'

'We try to be. Clarissa's always so busy. Are you one of these new-fangled househusbands I've read so much about?'

'No, not really, my wife and I just take it in turns to do the pick-up, although now you mention it, this is my second day on the trot. I'll have to have a word with her.'

'Oh, I see. What do you do?'

'I'm a plumber.'

'Oh really? I have a problem with one of my taps, could you come and fix it?'

'Of course.'

'Give me your number and I'll ring you to arrange a time.'

About a week later, I arranged to go and fix her bath tap. 'Just to warn you, my husband is home,' she said to me. 'Don't worry, he doesn't live here. I can't live with him any more; he's just impossible, especially when he's working. I need to be able to sleep, and he doesn't. So he's moved out and now he lives in the flat opposite. You might see him. He's forever getting under my feet. He's a terrible show-off, always trying to shock people. He isn't half as eccentric as he pretends to be. Attention is the currency he craves, so just ignore him. He's just a naughty child who failed to make it to maturity.'

I didn't really know what to say, so I didn't respond. She showed me into the bathroom, pointed out the offending tap and I busied myself with the bath panel. Just as I managed to liberate it from its fixings, her husband appeared in the doorway wearing a deerstalker, smoking a thick cigar and carrying an air rifle. 'Would you mind opening the window,' he whispered under his breath as he knelt down beside me. 'They're a damn nuisance,' he muttered quietly, poking the tip of the barrel out of the bay window. He took aim and fired. There was a tiny squeak and a small squirrel fell out of a tree and landed on the roof of the shed at the far end of the garden. He stood up immediately, terribly excited, and said, 'Hah! Got him! Serves him bloody well right for barking my buddleia. You wouldn't be a jolly good chap and dispose of that for me, would you? I usually fling them over the fence, but my neighbour is getting a bit angsty about it. You wouldn't mind dropping it off in the woods for me would you? I'd be terribly grateful,' and with that, he retreated out of the room.

When I finished fixing the tap, I went back into the front room and found Clarissa's mum tangled up in wads of wool. 'Would you mind holding out your hands,' she said, trying to untangle herself. 'It's just so much easier if I do it like this,' she went on, wrapping the wool between my outstretched hands. The tap hadn't taken me very long so I was happy to indulge her. 'It just keeps getting snagged. You don't mind, do you?' The room was full of half-finished paintings that were all hanging in the oddest places. One was two inches above the skirting-board, behind the sofa, and yet there was nothing else on the wall above it.

'Why did you hang that there?' I asked, trying to conceal my bafflement at the disconnected nature of her decorative displays.

'There was a hook,' she said, winding the wool between my splayed fingers.

A few weeks later, I was standing in the playground when Clarissa came rushing through the school gates, terribly flustered, carrying lots of scraps of paper. 'What are they?' I asked.

'Just some old recipes. I was going to hand them out.'

'Why?'

'For the cake sale.'

I looked blank.

'Some of the mums haven't got any cake recipes, so I thought I'd bring some in. My mum tells me you're a plumber?'

'Yes, that's right.'

'We're thinking about replacing our central-heating system.'

'Yes, she mentioned it, while I was helping her with her knitting.'

'We've been told the whole system needs to be power-flushed, whatever that is. Is that something you could do?'

'Yes.'

'The thing is, we're thinking of building an extension and I don't know whether we should wait and then do it all together? What do you think?'

'I suppose it depends how bad it is and when you think you'll do the extension.'

'I know. We really want to do it, but I don't think we can afford it.'

'I could come and have a look at it if you like?' I offered.

'Oh, really? That would be great. I've just got to hand these out. Can you hold on a minute?'

'I don't mean right now.'

'Oh, sorry, I thought you meant ...'

'Well, I suppose I could.'

'That would be amazing.'

'Don't you think most people will just buy a cake?'

'Oh, do you think so? I hadn't thought of that. Isn't that cheating?'

'Well, not really. As long as you provide a cake, that's all that matters, isn't it?'

'I suppose so. I've just been so busy. I haven't really had time to think. So you don't think anyone will want any of my grandma's old recipes? Oh, I feel so silly. I spent ages photocopying them. I think I'm going to hand them out anyway.'

'Do you want a hand?'

'That would be amazing. It'll be so much quicker if we both do it.'

'Okay,' I said, grabbing a handful of recipes and slowly walking round the playground.

'Would you like one of Clarissa's grandma's old cake recipes? It's for the cake sale next week?' I said, not quite believing what I was doing. All the other parents looked at us as if we'd gone completely mad. 'In case you don't have any cake recipes of your own,' said Clarissa, desperately trying to justify herself as everyone gave us strange sideways looks, then walked off whispering to their kids to stay away from our children.

Once everyone had left the playground, my daughter ran up to me and flung her arms around me.

'Do you want to go to Tabby's house?'

'Yes, please,' she said, letting go of me and grabbing Tabby's hand. 'You can show me your room.'

'I've got a new bunk bed,' said Tabby, suddenly running on ahead.

Clarissa and I chatted all the way back to her flat. It was like we had been best friends for years. When we arrived, she opened her front door and I literally gasped.

'Christ! Kids, don't touch anything. This happened to us last Christmas,' I said, surveying the carnage. 'You call the police and I'll try to see where they got in.'

'What's wrong?' she said, laughing. 'It's not that bad! It's a bit of mess, I grant you. I was in such a rush this morning, I didn't have time to tidy up. I wasn't expecting visitors.'

'Oh, I'm so sorry. I thought you'd been burgled.'

She burst out laughing and went into the kitchen to put the kettle on. There were dirty plates and bowls, clothes, books, files, pieces of paper, toys, CDs, videos and DVDs everywhere.

'How long have you lived here?'

'About three years. We bought it for the garden really. It's stunning, isn't it? So unusual to get a garden this size in London. We've got great plans. What we want is to build a two-storey extension onto the side. Then we'd move the kitchen into it, put another bedroom above it and turn the existing kitchen into another bedroom. That way we'd turn it from a two-bed into a four-bed, and the kids won't have to share.'

'When are you going to do it?'

'I don't know. We've asked the freeholder and he says he won't object, so we're in the process of getting some plans drawn up. Then, once we have them, we'll apply for planning permission.'

'Sounds expensive.'

'That's the problem,' she agreed. 'The architect thinks it might cost £100,000. We don't have anything like that. So, we might have to wait. My question is, should we change the central-heating system now, because what we have is terrible? Honestly, it's absolutely freezing in winter. Can it be designed in such a way that we can easily add onto it later, when we can afford to do the extension?'

'Yes, of course.'

'Okay, well, what we want to do is to replace all the radiators and move them all to different positions. We really like the big vertical radiators. What do you think of them? Are they any good?'

'Yes, they are. Do you have any pets?' I said, seeing something move underneath a blanket that had been discarded under the kitchen table.

'Two cats, but they're both pretty feral now. One of them has moved in with someone else down the road. I don't think it can stand the mess,' she said, smiling.

'I think there's something moving around in your kitchen.'

'Oh my God, really? Where?'

'Over there, underneath that blanket,' I said, as a cat's face appeared out of the end of the blanket.

'Thank God for that!' said Clarissa, laughing. 'You really got me. We had mice a couple of months ago. Right, that's it. I'm going to tidy up.'

'Would you like me to give you a hand? You can tell me what you want while we're doing it.'

'Okay, deal,' she said, donning the rubber gloves.

An hour later, we finally sat down.

'So, what do you think?'

'Yes, I can do it.'

'That's great. Can you give me a price and I'll talk to my husband about it? There is a chance that my mum and dad might help us to do the extension, in which case we might hang on and do it all together, but if you could let me know how much it would be to do it now, we can at least discuss it.'

'No problem, give me a couple of days and I'll get it over to you.'

I didn't hear anything from her for about a month. I didn't know whether to mention it or not when I saw her in the playground. I didn't want to appear too pushy or desperate, so I just left it and wrote it off. Then, just when I was sure it probably wasn't going to happen, she wrote back.

'We're so pleased you can do it for us. Just let us know when you can start. Clarissa.'

I responded immediately: 'Great! How about in three weeks? Can you hang on till then?'

'Yes, that's fine. It will give us time to buy the radiators. Any tips?'

'Look online, but don't buy anything yet. I might be able to get them cheaper. Just figure out what you like and then leave it to me.'

Three weeks later I arranged to pick Ryan up from the usual place. It was definitely a two-man job and Ryan was always available. He looked his usual vagrant self. He hadn't shaved and was still wearing the ripped T-shirt I'd told him to throw away three months earlier.

Ryan concentrated on rolling his Rizla. Even though it looked like he wasn't listening, that didn't dissuade me from telling him what we had to do. That was the routine. I told him about the job and he pretended not to listen.

'It's quite a big job, this one. It's a new central-heating system with seven new vertical radiators, hung in different locations from where the current radiators are. It's a ground-floor flat with concrete floors. I don't want to chase the floors because I'm worried about breaching the damp-proof course. This means it all needs to be surface pipework and since it is going to be on show, it needs to be neat. The boiler is going to be replaced and a new one installed, in the cellar this time. It's partially above ground, so we can get the flue out, but it's only accessible from the outside and it's only three feet high. We're going to replace almost all the pipework, so we're going to need a shitload of copper. Anyway, let's rip it all out today and then we'll have to figure out the best way to do it.'

'Fair enough,' said Ryan, swallowing two Nurofen, washed down with a half-empty, stale can of Coke, which he'd left in the van several weeks earlier.

Ryan couldn't believe it when we arrived. Clarissa came out with two mugs of filter coffee and two plates of croissants. 'When you've had your coffee, I've made pancakes with maple syrup, if you'd like some?'

'That would be amazing,' said Ryan, checking himself out in the wing mirror.

★ ★ ★ ★

After three days of being just the most amazing client, Clarissa came and sat down next to me, as she often did.

'I completely forgot that they are unveiling a statue of my grandfather next week in Milan, so unfortunately none of us will be around from tomorrow. Do you think that's going to be a problem?'

'No, I shouldn't think so. As long as we know where you want everything to go before you leave.'

'It also means I'm not going to be able to do the cake sale this weekend. Is there any chance you could do it for me? I'd be really ever so grateful.'

'To be honest, it's not really my thing, but I'll ask Jo if she could do it, if you like?'

'Oh, would you? Thank you so much. I feel so terrible for asking.'

'No problem, just leave it with me. I'll ask her tonight.'

The next morning, I pulled up outside Clarissa's and Ryan was already there. Ryan was never early. I almost didn't recognise him. He was clean shaven, he had clearly had a shower and he was even wearing deodorant!

'Are you all right?' I said, as he got into the van.

'Yeah, why?'

'You're wearing a clean pair of jeans that look like they've been ironed!'

'So what?'

'And a brand-new T-shirt!'

'So?'

'What's going on?'

'Nothing. Just thought I'd make an effort, that's all.'

'Why? You've never made an effort before.'

'No reason.'

'Is it because of Clarissa?'

'No!'

'She's married, you know?'

'It's nothing to do with her.'

'You've been wearing the same shitty jeans and ripped T-shirt for the last ten years, then suddenly you turn up looking like you're due in court and you expect me to believe you just thought you'd make an effort? Yeah, right!'

'It's nothing to do with her. I've got a date after work, that's all,' he said.

'Oh, really? Who with?'

'One of the Polish barmaids from The Heart of Hackney.'

'Wow! That's a turn-up for the books. Where are you going?'

'Don't know. I was thinking of Garfunkel's. I went there once, years back.'

'Fair enough. It's not the most romantic, but …'

'It's not like that. We're just going out. I haven't figured out what we're going to do yet.'

'How old is she?'

'Thirty-two.'

'Thirty-two! Jesus, Ryan! You're old enough to be her father.'

'No, I'm not. I'm only fifty.'

'Exactly! She's eighteen years younger than you.'

'So what?'

'If you had a kid when you were eighteen …'

'I did have a kid when I was eighteen.'

'Well, then, she's the same age.'

'I don't care. I haven't been out on a date in years.'

'What the hell are you going to do with a thirty-two-year-old?'

'Tottenham are playing tonight. I thought we could watch that.'

'You can't take her to the pub to watch the football.'

'Why not? She loves watching Tottenham.'

'She can do that at work.'

'I won't take her to The Heart of Hackney.'

'Look, its nothing to do with me. It's your life,' I said, laughing. 'I suppose you're going to want some money off me then?'

'Yes, a couple of hundred quid should do it. Take it out of me wages for this week.'

The next day, Clarissa left to go to Milan and Ryan (typically) didn't turn up for work. I should have known. Every time I paid him before the end of the week, he never turned up the next day. Usually because he went off on a bender, but this time it was different. This time he completely disappeared off the face of the planet. He didn't answer his phone or reply to any of my messages. It got to the point that I almost called the police. But given his possible IRA connections I didn't think he'd thank me for that. Then, a week later, he turned up at Clarissa's flat, looking like he hadn't slept for a week.

'What the hell happened to you?'

'I'll tell you later,' he sighed, re-lighting his half-smoked cigarette. 'So you're still doing the central heating system then?'

'Yes. No thanks to you! I've had to hang all the radiators and piped it all up on my own. It's been a fucking nightmare.'

'Sorry,' he said.

'What the fuck happened?'

'We went to Garfunkel's, then afterwards she asked me if I wanted to go back to hers.'

'And?'

'I've never known anything like it! She wouldn't leave me alone.'

'Are you trying to tell me that you've been at it for the last week?'

'I couldn't get away.'

'And you couldn't ring me?'

'I tried to, but my phone died.'

'You should have fucking called me!'

'I know. I'm sorry. She works shifts, three weeks on, then one week off. I'm absolutely bloody knackered. I've hardly slept. I thought I was going to have a bloody heart attack. I swear to God. It isn't like it used to be.'

'Aren't you a bit old for all that crap?'

'Damn right. What's wrong with going down the pub, drinking ten pints, talking shit to some bird, then taking her home, fumbling around on the couch for ten minutes, then passing out? That's how it was done in my day. None of this, "Now it's my turn!".'

'What does that mean?' I said, bursting out laughing.

'It's not funny. I'm fucking sore. She kept saying "I'm responsible for my own orgasm." Then she started ordering me about. "Do this!". "Do that!". I felt like I was back at school.'

'So, you're not going to see her again?'

'I didn't say that. It's different, that's all. Takes a bit of getting used to. My ex didn't have a clitoris, or at least I never found it.'

'All right, all right, that's enough, I get the picture. I'm still fucking pissed off with you. You should have fucking called me. But since the last time you got laid Val Doonican was in the charts, I'm prepared to forget it. As it happens, you've come back just in time. I can't hang the new boiler on my own and no one else is available until next week. But I'm not subbing you ever again, so don't even ask. But for fuck's sake, don't tell me what you got up to. I don't want to know. It's making me feel nauseous.'

The next few days went well. Ryan got there early and, once he'd recovered from his severe sexual exertions, he hung the new boiler and hooked it up to all the new pipework that I had done while he was off getting his end away. Everything was going to plan. I even ended up doing the cake sale, because Jo was too busy. I got to the last day and all we had to do was fill the system and fire it up. We got there early so that it would be finished and the flat would be nice and warm for when Clarissa got back that evening. So, after we'd had a quick cup of tea, I went outside, crawled into the cellar and started to fill the system, while Ryan stayed inside to bleed all the radiators and check for any leaks. Unfortunately, half-way through, Ryan's girlfriend called him in a right state because she had just been fired from The Heart of Hackney. She was so upset that Ryan left what he was doing and went outside with the phone to try to calm her down.

Meanwhile, I continued filling the system, unaware that he was no longer inside. I continued pumping more and more water into the system, until, after about five minutes, I noticed that I hadn't heard anything from him and the pressure gauge on the boiler still hadn't moved, which it should have done, given the amount of water that had surged into the system. So, I stopped what I was doing, crawled back out of the basement and went to see if everything was okay. Ryan was at the end of the garden screaming down his phone. Realising that he was in the middle of a domestic, I ignored him and went to check up on things for myself. It was only then that I realised that the front door was locked. I gesticulated to Ryan, but he ignored me, turned around and walked off to the other side of the garden. So, I looked through the letterbox and could see the keys sitting on the dining table in the lounge. I threw myself against the door with my shoulder, but it wouldn't budge. I stood back and started booting it as hard as I could, trying to break it down, but it still didn't move. I got out my credit card and tried to slip the safety catch, but the door was too tight against the frame. By this time I was feeling extremely anxious, so, as a last resort, because I was now imagining water pissing out all over the place inside, I ran as fast as I could to the local locksmiths. When I arrived, I threw up outside. The locksmith was also a cobbler, and he knew me. Seeing my distress, he quickly realised that it was an emergency and took pity on me. By this time, I was quite sure the whole place was under water. I jumped into his van and he drove me straight back to Clarissa's flat.

All the way back, I was trying to work out how I was going to tell Clarissa that her brand new wooden floors had been ruined. Within a few minutes of getting back, with the help of an ingenious mechanism which the locksmith inserted into the letter box, the door opened. I flew round that flat like a fireman running into a burning building. But there wasn't any water anywhere. Nothing. Not a single leak. I couldn't believe it. It didn't make any sense. It was the strangest feeling of intense relief, combined with full-on fury at Ryan. Just then, Ryan walked in. 'I think I might have left one of the bleed valves open,' he said, walking over to the largest and highest radiator and turning it off. When you're filling a heating system for the first time, you have to allow air to bleed from the lowest radiator first, closing bleed valves on each radiator progressively upwards so as to purge air from the system. Fortunately, Ryan had bled all the radiators apart from that one before his girlfriend called, and I stopped filling the system before that radiator was full, otherwise water would have been all over the floor.

'No wonder there wasn't any fucking pressure in the system,' I screamed. 'I've just run half-way across Haringey to get this guy to break in because you shut the bloody door and left the fucking keys inside. I honestly thought I'd flooded the place!'

'Sorry. I had no idea.'

'That's because you've been talking to your fucking girlfriend.'

'She's not my girlfriend any more. She's a right slapper.'

'For fuck's sake, Ryan, I don't care! If I'm outside filling a central-heating system, don't leave a bleed valve open and then fuck off and lock the door behind you. It could have been a complete fucking disaster! I'm going to have to lie down. Honestly, I'm feeling faint,' I said, walking outside and lying down on the grass.

Just then Clarissa arrived back, full of the joys of spring. 'Are you okay?' she said, opening her garden gate.

'Yes, I'm fine,' I said, jumping to my feet. 'I wasn't expecting you back till this evening.'

'We ended up getting on an earlier flight. Is everything okay?'

'Yes, we're just doing the final few tweaks and it will be ready for you.'

'Oh, it all looks so neat,' she said, carrying her bags inside. 'You've done such a good job. How did the cake sale go?'

'It was fine. I did it in the end. Jo was busy. I sold twenty-five cakes and lots of those chocolate cornflakey things. They were a hit.'

'Oh, I'm so pleased. Thank you so much.'

'How was the unveiling?'

'Wonderful! It was so special having everyone together. My cousins came all the way from Australia. It was a real family event.'

Twenty minutes later, the new boiler kicked in and all the new radiators started to warm up.

'It's already warmer than it ever used to be,' she said, putting her hands onto the top of one of the radiators. 'While we were in Milan, my mum offered to help us do the extension, so it looks like we might be doing it sooner than we thought.'

'That's great. Just let me know if there's anything else you need from me and I'll be happy to help. It's been an absolute joy working for you.'

'Thank you. You've done a brilliant job. Send me your invoice and I'll pay it straight away.' And that was it.

Or so I thought.

* * * *

Six months later, Clarissa called me in the middle of the night in a complete panic. 'Oh, thank God you've picked up. We've got water pouring through our ceiling! I don't know what to do. It's everywhere!'

'Okay, go into the kitchen and turn the stopcock off. It's in the corner underneath the kitchen sink.'

'Thank you so much. Okay, I'm in the kitchen now.'

'Look in the cupboard under the kitchen sink. In the left corner, can you see a brass fitting with a tap-like head on it?'

'Yes.'

'That turns the water off to the whole flat. Turn it clockwise until it won't turn any further.'

'Okay, I'm doing that … right … okay, it won't turn any more.'

'All right, that should stop it. You won't have any water tonight, but I'll be there first thing tomorrow morning to sort it out.'

'Okay, thank you so much. You couldn't pick up a pint of milk, could you? So I can make you a cup of tea.'

'No problem.'

Twenty minutes later my phone rang again.

'It hasn't stopped. It's still pouring through the ceiling.'

'Okay, I'm on my way.'

There was at least two inches of water throughout the whole flat when I got there. 'It's coming from the flat upstairs,' I said, relieved that it wasn't anything I had done.

'We thought it might be, but he's away at the moment. We've tried ringing him, but he isn't answering and he isn't getting back to us. He's the freeholder for the whole building and also lives upstairs.'

'Have you got any keys?'

'No, we don't really know him.'

'Has anyone else got any keys?'

'No, I don't think so.'

'Okay, I can turn the water off to the whole building, but then no one in any of the flats will have any water. I'll go and explain what's happened and tell them what I'm going to do.'

I started ringing on all the other doorbells, but no one answered.

'Typical London. Look, don't worry, I'll turn it off anyway.'

The next day, I went back at 7 a.m., with a pint of milk so Clarissa could make me a cup of tea. The owners of all the other flats were absolutely furious. Several of them had already called Thames Water to complain. The owner of the flat directly above Clarissa's still hadn't returned any of her calls, so I couldn't turn the water back on. After several screaming matches and a bit of argy-bargy between Clarissa and some of the other flat owners, I called the cobbler/locksmith and he came around and helped me break in. When he drove up, things were getting quite heated. The owner of the second floor flat was being particularly belligerent. The cobbler was an intimidatingly large man, with tattoos of naked women with big boobs down both of his arms. He looked like a giant circus strongman, better suited to fighting in fairgrounds than working behind a counter in a shoe shop. Nevertheless, his arrival seemed to bring peace to the proceedings and the belligerent bastard from the second floor finally shut up and left. 'I'm not supposed to do this, you know,' he said, delicately drilling the lock. 'But since it's you, I'll make an exception.' Once we were in, it was immediately clear what had happened. The inlet valve to the toilet had broken and the overflow wasn't connected, so the water was pouring out onto the floor. I isolated the water to the toilet, then turned the water back on outside.

A week later, the owner of the flat came back from holiday and couldn't get into his flat because we'd changed the locks. Clarissa had left a letter pinned to his front door explaining what had happened. But she hadn't enclosed the keys, in case someone broke in. Unfortunately, she was out when he got back. When she got home, he was sitting on the steps with all his bags. She explained what happened after that:

'Oh, I'm so sorry. How long have you been waiting?' she said, sheepishly stretching out her hand to welcome him back.

'I've been here for about three hours,' he replied, ignoring her attempts to shake his hand. His eyes were cold and he was clearly furious.

'Did you get my note?' said Clarissa, trying to ease the tension. 'There was a leak in your flat and we've made an insurance claim. They're going to contact you.'

'Yes. Can I have the keys to my flat?'

'Of course. I'm so sorry. I've been waiting in for the last week. I had no idea when you were getting back. Have you been anywhere nice?'

'Australia. I've just got off a twenty-four-hour flight and I didn't get any sleep on the plane.'

Clarissa gave him the keys and he disappeared upstairs. Five minutes later he came back down and banged on her door. 'The toilet isn't working.'

'Yes, that's right. That's what caused the leak. We had to get our plumber to disconnect it. Here's his number. I'm sure he'll be happy to come and fix it for you.'

Two minutes later, he called me and I went around immediately. When I got there, he completely lost it. 'Let me get this right. There was a leak in my flat that was dripping into the flat downstairs,' he said, marching up and down outside the bathroom.

'It was a little bit more than a drip.'

'Whatever. So, you broke in and disconnected my toilet. Is that right?'

'Well no, not quite. I turned the water off to the whole building first, but that meant nobody in the building had any water. Clarissa tried to get in contact with you, but no one responded and since there's no way to turn the water off just to your flat, we didn't have any other option.'

'So you broke in!'

'Yes.'

'That's breaking and entering.'

'Not really. What was I supposed to do? There was water pissing through the ceiling downstairs.'

'How do I know you didn't steal anything?'

'I'm hardly likely to return to the scene of the crime if I burgled the place.'

'I'm calling the police.'

'I realise you're tired, but don't you think you're being a little bit irrational?'

'Irrational! You broke into my fucking flat and disconnected my bloody toilet!'

'I'll tell you what, I'll fix it now, but for goodness sake, don't call the police.'

'I'm not fucking paying you.'

'Fine.'

'Okay,' he said, marching into the other room.

About a year later, Clarissa called me.

'Hi Nick, it's Clarissa.'

'Clarissa! How are you? How's the extension?'

'Oh, didn't you hear? We ended up having a complete nightmare with the freeholder. He owned the flat upstairs.'

'Not the one that flooded your flat?'

'Yes! Do you remember?'

'How could I forget?'

'He turned out to be a really nasty piece of work.'

'Yes, I know,' I recalled how he'd threatened me with the police when I'd done him a big favour. 'What happened?'

'Well, once we'd got the plans drawn up, we showed them to him and he said he was fine with it. So, after we got planning permission, put it out to tender and chose a builder, we moved out. It made sense to do it at the same time as we repaired the damage from the flood. The insurance company messed us around for ages, but eventually they agreed to cough up.'

'So have you done it, then? I'll have to come round and have a look.'

'No. Right at the last minute, literally the day before the builders were about to start, the freeholder, the man in the upstairs flat, demanded £100,000 to sign it off.'

'No way!'

'And the awful thing was, the law was on his side. As a freeholder, he could charge whatever he wanted. There was no way we could afford to pay him that as well as do the extension. We tried to fight him, but it was no good. He wouldn't even negotiate. Eventually, it became clear that all we were doing was lining the lawyer's pockets, so we had no option but to fix it up and sell it. We couldn't stay there after that, which is why I'm calling.'

'Don't tell me. You've found a new place and you want a brand-new heating system?'

'No, not quite. I was just wondering if you could come and look at the place we are thinking of buying and let us know if there is anything wrong with it?'

'Of course, but aren't you getting a survey?'

'Yes, but they just cover their own arse. I want to know from someone I trust.'

'Sure,' I said. 'How about 10.30 tomorrow morning?'

'That would be great. I'll just have to check with the estate agent. Oh, I have a meeting at nine and then I have a fitness class straight after, but I should be back by 10.30.'

'Let's make it 12,' I said, smiling.

'Okay, I'll get the estate agent to meet us there.'

'Great. Text me the address.'

'Oh, and Nick, if we do buy it, I want to put one of those vertical radiators into the study.'

* * * *

Jo and Clarissa became close friends after that, and we started to see her socially. Fifteen years passed. Our kids grew up; we all lost our parents; and the squirrel population of north London boomed. Clarissa bounced back, and is now living in a lovely house in Leyton. And guess what? She owns the freehold.

Then, out of the blue, in the middle of the pandemic lockdown, my phone rang. It was the freeholder of Clarissa's old flat. 'I've got water pouring through my ceiling,' he said. 'I've tried at least ten plumbers and no one's available!'

'Really?' I said, realising who it was.

'It's coming from the flat upstairs. No one's in and I don't know where to turn the water off.'

Several days later, Jo went for a walk with Clarissa and told her what had happened. Her eyes lit up. 'What did Nick do?' she said, desperately trying to contain her curiosity.

'He told him to call the police.'

'He didn't!'

'He did,' she said, laughing. 'What goes around, comes around.'

Clarissa burst into tears. 'I know it's silly. I'm so over it now. It's ancient history, really. But he shouldn't have been allowed to do what he did. I'm not one to hold grudges. It isn't healthy. But I'm glad Nick did that. He's a real hero, your husband. Thank you for telling me. I'm pleased that man finally got his comeuppance.' That evening, when I got back from work, Jo told me what Clarissa had said. I laughed and took out my little black book. On the page marked Clarissa, underneath dead-squirrel remover, knitting helper, recipe distributor, cleaner, cake-sale organiser, accessory to breaking and entering, milkman, fixer of neighbour's toilet and property surveyor, I drew a tiny picture of a man wearing a mask and a cape, with a P on his chest, and underneath that I wrote three words: 'Justice on tap.'

Who's the Villain?

No one wants to be the villain in their own story, but sometimes it simply can't be helped. Several years ago, I had a day like no other. It felt as if I had inadvertently strayed into *The Twilight Zone*. I realise now that my actions can be interpreted in lots of different ways. Some people see the good, while others see the bad. Which side they choose says as much about them as it does about me, but once they've chosen their side, there is nothing I can do to change their minds, even if I feel they're being grossly unfair. This is my attempt to set the record straight.

It was early February 2015. Jo and I were supposed to be going to the premiere of *Fifty Shades of Grey* in Leicester Square. A close friend of ours had worked on it and had got us tickets. We were both really excited about it. I had never been to a premiere before. But I had a full day's work to do first. Winter was in full swing, the heating had been on for months and snow was starting to fall as I made my way to my van that morning. I was rubbing my hands together in an attempt to keep warm as I scraped the ice off my windscreen and the lyrics from *Oliver!*, 'In this life, one thing counts, in the bank, large amounts', jumped into my head as I pondered the prospect of lots of frozen pipes.

I started early. My first client was an extremely highly-strung middle-aged woman with a tight bob and a slight lisp. She had clearly drunk far too much coffee before I arrived. She answered the door before I had even knocked and immediately held her finger to her lips. 'My son is just back from uni,' she whispered. 'He didn't get back until very late last night. Can you change the kitchen tap first and then do the toilet upstairs? The bathroom is next to his bedroom, so please try to be as quiet as you can. He's always been an incredibly light sleeper. As a child he used to sleep on my breast because I couldn't get him off without waking him up. Oh, my word! Is that the time? I'm late! Help yourself to tea and coffee. It's in the cupboard above the kettle. There's milk in the fridge. Thank you so much for coming. Just text me when you're done, and I'll transfer the funds when I get home this evening. Thanks again.' And with that, she quietly closed the door and started running down the road towards the bus stop. A few minutes later, I heard the bed upstairs start to creak. After a while it started to tap against the wall, slowly at first, and then quickly picking up momentum. I zoned it out and tried to focus in on the tap. Clearly there was shagging going on upstairs, which was none of my business.

I quietly closed the kitchen door and carried on. But the knocking gradually built and built until I couldn't ignore it any more. Then, there was a sudden crash and laughing. I imagined they must have fallen off the bed. After about a minute, they jumped back onto the bed and started again. It was extremely distracting. I didn't know whether I should make a loud noise to warn them that I was there, or just carry on regardless and hope they would burn themselves out. After about half an hour, I had finished changing the kitchen tap, so I carefully crept up the stairs and bolted the bathroom door once I was inside. By this time, it was quiet and I was quite sure that they must both have fallen asleep, worn out from their earlier escapades.

I quietly started to dismantle the toilet. When I was half-way through fixing the loo, I heard some movement in the bedroom next door. My heart sank. I stopped what I was doing and sat there, motionless, waiting for things to quieten down. I felt like I was trying to break out of prison and I'd just heard a guard walking down the corridor towards my cell. About a minute later, there was silence. I presumed they had just rolled over and gone back to sleep. So, I carried on tightening up the wingnuts. Then, just as I'd finished securing the cistern to the wall, I heard movement again next door followed by a great big bang up against the other side of the bathroom wall, next to where I was crouching. I didn't know what to do with myself. I was literally right next door. I didn't know whether I should leave and come back later, or just ignore them, like I had tried to do before.

I had a full day's work lined up, so I couldn't easily leave and come back later, because all my other work was miles away. Anyway, I was already half-way through the job. So, I kept my head down, stayed quiet and quickly finished putting the toilet back together. This time things were a lot less manic; they were taking their time. It was going to be a marathon, rather than a sprint. They were clearly taking full advantage of his mum not being in. Enduring this was like water torture. Slow and methodical, but with maximum mental torment guaranteed. Then, just after it finally subsided, the bedroom door opened and I heard her say, 'I need a wee.' Light footsteps flitted over the floorboards towards the bathroom. I panicked and started looking for somewhere to hide. In the shower perhaps? Or maybe I should lie down in the bath? No, she would see me. Or should I just come clean and open the bathroom door to warn her that I was in there? In the end, I ran out of time to decide and I simply bent over the toilet and started fiddling with the wingnuts again at the back of the cistern. 'Don't move, I'll be right back,' I heard her say, as she tried to push the bathroom door open with her foot.

'It's all fixed,' I said, unbolting the door. 'I've put a new kitchen tap in for you downstairs as well.' She was draped in his dressing gown, had clearly been sweating and her hair was dishevelled. She looked at me with absolute horror, turned round and ran straight back into the bedroom. 'You told me there was no one in the house, you bastard!' she screamed, as I quickly flushed the loo, to check it wasn't leaking, gathered my tools and left.

★ ★ ★ ★

My next job was for an old lady called Mavis who had just received an astronomical water bill. She lived in a private cul-de-sac in Harrow on the Hill, not far from the famous school. In fact, her road ran parallel to some of the school's playing fields. When I got there, the barrier was up, so I drove straight down the boulevard of bungalows with their neatly tended front gardens until I came to her house. Workmen were pollarding the plane trees that lined the side of the road as the schoolboys hurried out of their houses in their distinctive dark-blue jackets and light-grey trousers, on their way to their early morning worship. I knocked on the front door, but no one answered. So, I called her to check that I'd got the right address, but still no one answered. I sent a text telling her I was outside. Ten minutes later, the door opened and an elderly woman appeared in the doorway, with white hair that had been coloured with a light-blue rinse. She was wearing a dark-blue tabard and was carrying a miniature doll's-house chair. 'Are you the plumber?' she said sweetly, as her eyes clouded over. She seemed to be distracted by something in the distance. I turned around, but there was nothing there, so I carried on.

'Yes,' I said.

'I beg your pardon?' she said, squinting at me suspiciously.

'YES,' I shouted back.

'You'll have to excuse me, I'm slightly hard of hearing,' she said, pointing the volume control for her hearing aid at me, as if she was turning me up. 'Why didn't you ring the bell?'

'I did.'

'Really? I didn't hear a thing. Anyway, you're here now. I've had a bill,' she said, putting the tiny chair down on the table next to the front door. 'Come in. Don't linger on the doorstep! Through here,' she said, showing me into the kitchen. On the table was the most beautiful light-blue Victorian doll's house. It was almost the exact colour of her hair. 'That's gorgeous,' I said, complimenting her craftsmanship.

'I've made bigger!' she said.

'NO, IT'S GORGEOUS,' I shouted.

'It's no such thing. It's a doll's house. They are by definition small. That's why I make them.'

'GORGEOUS!'

'I thought you said it was enormous,' she said, laughing. 'Now, where's that chair?'

'It's on the table.'

'It's nothing of the sort. It's very stable.'

'THE CHAIR IS ON THE TABLE BY THE FRONT DOOR.'

'A terrible bore! Not at all. I've been making them for years.'

'SHALL I GET IT FOR YOU?'

'Get what?'

'The chair?' I walked out of the kitchen and picked up the tiny chair and brought it back.

'That's where it went. I thought I'd lost you,' she said, taking it and delicately placing it in the front room of the doll's house.

'I SEE IT'S GOT ELECTRICITY IN IT,' I shouted, pointing to the lights it had in every room.

'Yes, I suppose I am,' she replied.

It felt like we were communicating in completely different dialects. 'ELECTRICITY,' I yelled.

'You'll have to excuse me, my hearing aids are playing up,' she said, pointing the remote at me again. 'I lip-read as well, so please look at me when you're talking to me. And don't slur your words, otherwise I'll get the wrong end of the stick.'

'ELECTRICITY.'

'I thought you said "eccentricity". There's no need to treat me like an imbecile, just speak clearly, that's all.'

'Okay,' I shouted, looking straight at her.

'Good, I've had a bill. Let me find it. I had it here just a minute ago. Ah, here it is. It's from Thames Water. They are trying to charge me over £1,000! It's outrageous. I called them and told them that I haven't been using any more water than I usually do.'

'WHAT DID THEY SAY?'

'I couldn't understand a word he was saying.'

'YOU MIGHT HAVE A LEAK?'

'I agree, hell of a cheek!'

'NO, I SAID YOU MIGHT HAVE A LEAK.'

'No, I don't think he was Greek. Sounded more Indian to me.'

'HAVE YOU SEEN ANY EVIDENCE OF A LEAK ANYWHERE?'

'A leak? No. I'd have called a plumber if I had a leak. I told them that, when I was on the phone.'

'I AM A PLUMBER – IS THAT NOT WHY YOU CALLED ME? WHY DON'T YOU SHOW ME AROUND?'

'That's precisely what I said. It's probably underground.' She showed me into her hallway.

'HAVE YOU LEFT A TAP ON?'

'No. Why?'

'ARE YOU SURE?'

'Yes, of course I'm sure. I'm not in the habit of leaving taps on.'

'IT SOUNDS LIKE YOU'VE LEFT A TAP ON. WHERE IS THE BATHROOM?'

'Bathroom? It's through there.'

'APART FROM THE KITCHEN, IS THIS THE ONLY OTHER ROOM THAT HAS WATER IN IT?' I shouted, looking straight at her as I pointed to the bathroom.

'Yes, I think so.'

'Okay,' I said, looking around the bathroom. 'I CAN HEAR WATER RUNNING. IT'S REALLY LOUD! CAN'T YOU HEAR IT?'

'No, I can't hear a thing.'

'You can say that again,' I whispered to myself.

'OKAY, I'M GOING TO TURN THE WATER OFF OUTSIDE. YOU'VE GOT A LEAK UNDER THE FLOOR. I THINK IT'S UNDER THE LOUNGE.'

'Well, do what you have to do,' she said, walking back into the kitchen to do something else to the doll's house.

I turned the water off outside, rolled the carpet back, lifted a couple of floorboards and felt the pipe that ran into the bathroom. It had split and water was still seeping out. I pointed my torch onto the ground underneath the house and then sat back on the floor. There was no ground left. Just water for as far as I could see. I went outside and turned the water back on and then I ran back into the house. Water was pissing out of the pipe. I bolted back outside and turned it off. Then I got a rod, which I normally use to unblock drains, from my van so I could measure how deep the water was under the house. The rod was three feet. I took it back into the house and poked it down into the hole. She had a shallow swimming pool under there. No wonder she'd had a huge bill. It must have been like that for months.

'YOU'VE GOT A LEAK UNDER THE FLOOR. IT'S ON THE MAIN. IT'S SPLIT. THERE IS A LOT OF WATER UNDERNEATH YOUR HOUSE. I'M GOING TO FIX IT.'

'I don't want another visit.'

'NO, FIX IT! *I'M GOING TO FIX IT.*'

'Good. I should think so!'

A couple of hours later, I packed my tools away and went to tell her that it was all fine. When I went back into the kitchen, she was standing on a stool trying to change a lightbulb. 'LET ME DO THAT FOR YOU,' I shouted, worrying that she was going to fall.

'Thank you,' she said, getting down off the stool and handing me the lightbulb. 'So much easier changing a lightbulb in there,' she said, pointing to the doll's house.

'DO YOU SELL THEM? YOUR DOLL'S HOUSES, I MEAN? I'M THINKING OF BUYING ONE FOR MY DAUGHTER.'

'Well, this one is really quite intricate. It's got lights and everything. It took me ages to put it together. I buy them as a kit and then I put the pieces together, slowly. It's a bit like a jigsaw.'

'YES, I CAN SEE THAT.'

'How much do I owe you?'

'THAT'S BEEN TWO HOURS PLUS MATERIALS, SO £175.'

'I don't have any money. Can I give you a cheque?'

'YES, OF COURSE.'

'Now, where is it? I'm sure I put it down somewhere.'

'IF YOU'D PREFER, WE COULD SWAP. I WON'T CHARGE YOU FOR FIXING YOUR LEAK AND YOU COULD GIVE ME THIS BEAUTIFUL DOLL'S HOUSE? WE COULD DO A TRADE IF THAT WOULD BE EASIER?'

'You want to buy my doll's house?'

'YES. IN A MANNER OF SPEAKING.'

'I thought you said it was enormous.'

'NO, I SAID IT WAS GORGEOUS.'

'Oh well, in that case … Do you want to see the other ones I've made? I've got lots of others.'

'NO, I'M FINE. I THINK MY DAUGHTER WOULD LOVE THIS ONE.'

'How old is she?'

'SEVEN.'

'Okay. I just need to finish it. It shouldn't take me long. While you are here, my friend needs to get her boiler serviced. Would you be able to have a look?'

'YES, NO PROBLEM. WHAT NUMBER IS SHE?'

'Fifteen. Right next door. Her name is Doris. She'll be pleased as punch.'

'OKAY, I'LL GO AND DO THAT. THEN I'LL COME BACK AND PICK UP THE DOLL'S HOUSE AFTER YOU'VE FINISHED IT.'

I put my tools into the back of my van and walked over to number fifteen. I looked out over the playing fields where the offspring of property developers and politicians were trying to prove themselves on the rugby pitches. I rang the doorbell and heard a bit of a kerfuffle inside. Then Doris came to the door, dressed in a bright-pink towelling tracksuit, with her knickers on the outside of her trousers, a thick, dark-blue duffle coat, a maroon scarf wrapped tightly round her neck, and a Second World War sheepskin flying hat on her head. 'Are you the plumber?' she said, shivering.

'Yes, I've come to have a look at your boiler,' I replied.

'Good, it seems to be on the blink. I can't seem to get it going. They keep telling me I need to get a new one, but I don't see why. It's fine, it just needs a service, that's all. Come in, come in, no use standing around out there,' she said, ushering me inside.

'Where is it?'

'Where's what?'

'The boiler?'

'Oh yes, of course, well that's just it. I don't know. I can't find it. It used to be in the cupboard in the kitchen, but it's not there any more. I think it's been moved.'

'Where to?'

'That's just it. I have absolutely no idea. I can't find it. As a plumber, is there a special way of finding boilers?'

'No, not really.'

'Well, how on earth do you fix them, if you can't find them first?'

'Most people tend to know where their boiler is.'

'I dare say they do, but I don't. As I said, it's been moved.'

'Can you show me where it used to be?'

'Yes, it used to be in here,' she said, showing me into the kitchen and opening a large louvred door.

'Yes, I can see that,' I said, looking at lots of open heating pipes, which had clearly once been attached to a boiler. 'But it's not here now,' I pointed out.

'I can see that. As I keep saying, it's been moved.'

'Yes. And you don't know where to?'

'No.'

'Are you sure it's been moved? It's just it's very unusual that they didn't cap these pipes. You see, they've left them open,' I said, pointing to the flow and return. How many radiators do you have?'

'I have no idea. They're utterly useless. They never warm up. Can you have a look at those for me? I think they need servicing too.'

'So how do you keep warm?'

'Fan heaters, mostly. I've got an electric fire in the lounge.'

'What about hot water?'

'Oh, I have plenty of hot water.'

'Do you have a hot-water tank?'

'Yes. It's upstairs in the cupboard on the landing.'

'Can I see it?'

'Do you think they might have put the boiler in there?'

'Possibly.'

'What would it look like?'

She showed me upstairs and opened the cupboard. Inside was an old hot-water tank with an immersion heater wired into the top of it. I followed the wire to a switch on the wall and saw that it was switched on. 'You're heating your hot water with an immersion heater.'

'What does that mean?'

'It means your hot water isn't being heated by your boiler.'

'I don't understand.'

'Can you show me some of the radiators?'

I bent down and felt the radiator in the hall. It was absolutely freezing. 'Are all your radiators this cold?' I asked her.

She walked over and put her hand on it. 'Actually, that's a bit warmer than most of the others.'

'Doris, I'm sorry to say this,' I explained, 'but I don't think you've got a boiler.'

'I don't understand.'

'I think it's been removed and hasn't been replaced. You don't remember anyone coming to talk to you about it?'

'Yes, of course, I do. I paid someone over £3,500 to replace it.'

'Why don't you call him?'

'I have. He never picks up his phone and doesn't return any of my calls.'

'I think that's because he's taken out your old boiler and he hasn't replaced it.'

'He told me he was going to move it out of the kitchen. But it would be fine to keep turning it on and off with the thermostat in the hall.'

'I bet he did. Honestly, I don't think he's replaced it.'

'So do the radiators need servicing?'

'No, the radiators are probably fine, you just need a new boiler. Would you like me to give you a price to install one for you? It's the middle of winter. I wouldn't recommend living here without one. I'm sorry to tell you this, Doris, but I think you may have been the victim of a conman.'

Just then, there was a knock at the door. Doris shuffled over to the front door and opened it. On the front doorstep was a tall man in British Gas overalls, and next to him on the floor was a large box. 'Hi Doris, I've got your new boiler. I don't think we're going to need to move it after all. I've measured it and I think it will fit just fine into that cupboard in the kitchen.'

'When did she order it?' I enquired, somewhat suspiciously.

'Yesterday. I've just been waiting for it to arrive.'

'When did you take the old boiler out?'

'Yesterday.'

'Really?'

'Yes.'

'Fair enough. Well it looks like this nice young man is going to put a new boiler in for you today, Doris, so I'll be on my way.'

Doris looked confused and didn't say anything, then she walked into the other room. As I walked back to Mavis's house, a gentle rain began to fall, coating my clothes and skin with a thin film of water. I knocked on the door. Again, no one answered, so I texted her and a few minutes later, Mavis appeared, wearing jodhpurs, a long red coat and a riding hat.

'IT'S OKAY, SOMEONE'S JUST ARRIVED TO INSTALL A NEW BOILER FOR HER.'

'I beg your pardon.'

'YOUR NEIGHBOUR, DORIS. SOMEONE'S JUST ARRIVED TO INSTALL A NEW BOILER FOR HER.'

'I don't know what you're talking about.'

'DORIS. YOU SAID SHE NEEDED SOMEONE TO SERVICE HER BOILER.'

'I said no such thing. Boris has been dead for years.'

'NO. DORIS! NEXT DOOR.'

'Are you telling me I don't know my own brother?'

'NEVER MIND. IS THE DOLL'S HOUSE READY?'

'What doll's house?'

'THE ONE I BOUGHT OFF YOU FOR MY DAUGHTER.'

'I don't know what you're talking about. I don't sell my doll's houses. I make them for my grandchildren.'

'BUT I FIXED A LEAK FOR YOU IN EXCHANGE FOR THE ONE IN YOUR KITCHEN.'

'You did no such thing. I've never seen you before in my life. I don't want a new boiler. I've already got one. Please leave me alone or I'll call the police.' Then she closed the door. I stood there not quite knowing what to do. Just then the British Gas man came out of the house next door.

'Excuse me,' I said, walking over to him, 'Have you noticed that something's not right here? I just fixed a leak for this lady and she asked me to go and help her neighbour and then when I got back, she doesn't seem to know who I am.'

'You mean, you don't know?'

'Know what?'

'They've all got dementia here,' he told me. 'It's a gated community. You shouldn't be dealing with them directly. There's a warden who oversees the whole development. He's the one who sorts out any payments etc.'

'Really? I had no idea.'

'I'd recommend you go and talk to him.'

I wandered down to the warden's office and explained the situation. While I was there, Mavis appeared at the window in her riding hat, carrying a riding crop.

'She thinks she's going riding,' said the warden. 'You're lucky, the woman at number twenty tries to breastfeed her dolls. It's not a pretty sight. I'm sorry, I believe you. I'm sure you did fix a leak for her, and that you did agree to waive your charge in exchange for one of her doll's houses, but you must understand it's your word against hers and unless you can prove it, there's really nothing I can do.'

'But there's a shallow swimming pool under her house.'

'I'm sure there is, but you should have come to see me first.'

I walked out of his office and an old man whom I'd never met before came up to me and said, 'You've grown a beard!'

'Yes,' I replied.

'You look much better with a beard. Much more distinguished.'

'Thank you,' I replied.

'Are you still fishing?'

'No, not so much.'

'That's a shame. You used to be such a wonderful fisherman. What was that fly you used to use?'

'I'm sorry, I think you must have got me mixed up with someone else.'

'Barnaby, is that you?' he said, walking off. Then he stopped and started to take his trousers off. At that moment, a man ran out of a nearby bungalow and escorted him back up the road, while the boys continued to play rugby in the rain on Harrow's playing fields.

★ ★ ★ ★

As I arrived at my van, my phone rang. 'Hi, is that the plumber? You don't know me, my name is Lisa, you've been recommended to me by a friend, Juliet Barton, she lives next door to me in Muswell Hill.'

'Yes, I know Juliet.'

'She said you might be able to help me. I have four children under seven, so, as you can imagine, it's a bit of a madhouse here. Anyway, one of them has drawn all over the side of our brand-new stone bath with crayons. I've tried everything to get it off, but I just can't shift it. Juliet said you might be able to help.'

'As it happens, I'm going to be driving past your house in about half an hour. Text me your address and I'll swing by and take a look.'

'That would be amazing.'

Half an hour later, I pulled into Lisa's driveway and slowly walked up the steep steps to the front door. After a loud clatter and a lot of screaming, the door finally opened. 'Are you the plumber?' she said, holding a screaming baby in her arms. She looked utterly exhausted. She had bags under her eyes and looked like she was about to have a nervous breakdown. 'Sometimes I think I'm going mad. Is it normal to hate your children?' she said, inviting me in. 'All they do is fight.'

'Having four kids is enough to drive anyone mad,' I said, trying to console her.

'Have you got any kids?'

'Yes, two, and that's bad enough. I don't know anyone who's had four and hasn't come close to cracking up.'

'I've got five. I've also got a teenage daughter.'

'How old is she?'

'Nearly sixteen'

'That's tough. They all go a bit loopy at that age.'

'Tell me about it. She's completely out of control. Doesn't come home. Is out all night doing God knows what! It's a miracle I'm still sane.'

I looked at her. She was still sane. Just. She was right on the edge. But there was a calmness to her. She was almost too calm. It didn't properly correlate with what she was saying. I felt as if she might suddenly snap and burst into tears at any moment. Or suddenly start screaming. Just then, an arrow flew out of the kitchen door and stuck on the wall just behind her head. 'Lottie, I told you not to fire that inside,' she said, turning around and rushing back into the kitchen just as the baby began to be sick.

'He said I was fat!' came a voice from the kitchen.

'Jonny, don't call her fat.'

'Put that down!'

Just then, a dart came flying down the stairs and embedded itself in the parquet floor next to my foot.

'I'm terribly sorry. James, stop throwing those darts! You could kill someone!'

'Give me that back,' screamed Lottie.

'No, it's mine. You've had your turn.'

'STOP FIGHTING,' shouted Lisa, grabbing the bow and arrow as she tried to wipe the baby's face. 'Neither of you can have it.'

'That's not fair! She had loads of goes!'

'ENOUGH! I'm so sorry. Just let me put the telly on and then I'll be right with you. James, come down, I'm putting *Dora the Explorer* on.' There was a clatter of feet followed by a loud bang as James came flying down the stairs, missing out every other step.

'Don't jump on the stairs,' she said, pressing the remote. James raced into the living room as *Dora the Explorer* came on and peace finally descended on the house. Lisa appeared in the doorway, looking like she was about to cry. 'I'm so sorry. They're just impossible. Let me show you the bath. It's up here,' she said, showing me up the stairs. 'Right to the top. On the left. We thought we'd splash out and got a free-standing stone bath. It was very expensive. I love it. Anyway, Lottie got some new crayons for her birthday and decided to draw all over it.' She opened the door and showed me. It was completely covered.

'She must have been at it for a while,' I said, kneeling down to survey the damage.

'Yes, I was on the phone to my mum. I thought she was playing in her room.'

'Okay. I can probably get it off, but it'll take me an hour, maybe longer.'

'When can you do it?'

'I can do it now if you like.'

'That would be great. How much will it be?'

'Between seventy and a hundred pounds.'

'That's fine. Can I leave you to it?'

'Yes, don't worry about me. I'll let you know when I'm done.'

'That's wonderful, thank you so much.'

Half an hour later, I heard the front door slam and the screaming started. Two women were tearing strips off each other downstairs. I couldn't hear all of it, only the bits that were screamed, though that was most of it.

'I can't believe you're doing this!'

'I'm allowed to say no!'

'It's just so unfair!'

'You're wrong! I don't want to hear it!'

'Why are you doing this?'

'You're sending me over the edge!'

'You don't understand! You'll never understand!'

'How dare you put me in this position!'

'You're driving me insane! You're killing me. You're literally killing me!'

This went on and on for at least an hour, possibly longer. It was still going on when I finally finished cleaning the crayons off the side of the bath. I cautiously came down the stairs and gently knocked on the kitchen door. The door flew open and Lisa stood there with tears running down her face.

'Sorry, can you please leave us alone.'

'Of course, I just thought I'd let you know it's done,' I replied.

'Thank you. Let me know how much and text me your bank details and I'll transfer you the money.' Just then, I realised that the girl she was arguing with was the same girl I'd encountered earlier. The one who had been shagging her boyfriend while I was in the bathroom next door. I stared at her and she stared at me, before she suddenly realised where she'd seen me before. 'You!' she screamed, pushing past me and running up the stairs.

When I got home, Jo was already dressed up and ready to go.

'I've finished doing the accounts. We had a very good year. We made fifteen per cent more than we did last year.'

'That's great! We should celebrate. Let's go out for dinner.'

'So that means we're going to have a massive tax bill and have to pay The Royal Ballet School even more.'

'Oh shit! Maybe not.'

'Exactly. Anyway, go and have a shower. We've got to leave in fifteen minutes. How was your day?'

'I went from shagging teenagers, to lost-it geriatrics to a mother on the edge of a nervous breakdown. It was all very surreal.'

'It could have been worse. It could have been the other way round: lost-it teenagers and shagging geriatrics!'

'True, that probably would have been worse, but only marginally.'

★ ★ ★ ★

It was dark when we arrived in Leicester Square and met up with our friends. We walked down the grey carpet that led up to the front door of the cinema, where the paparazzi waited. It was all very exciting. We took our seats and a few minutes before the film began the movie stars – Dakota

Johnson and Jamie Dornan – came in and sat down just three rows in front of us. All very thrilling. Then, about halfway through, came the scene in which Ana Steele gets undressed and takes a bath. It's the first time she is seen naked. The whole cinema held its breath as she stripped off and walked slowly over to the bath. At that moment, I turned to Jo and whispered, slightly louder than I had intended, 'That's exactly the same as the bath I was working on earlier!' Jo laughed and whispered, 'It's a sad state of affairs that in the most erotic scene of the film your focus is on the bath and not the woman, although I have to say I'm quite relieved!'

The next day I woke up slightly hung-over. Once I'd had a Berocca and cup of tea, I composed three texts to the people I'd done work for the previous day, requesting payment.

These were the responses I received:

'My son tells me you were very rude to both him and his girlfriend and that you listened in on them while they were having sex. I'm surprised you have the audacity to ask to be paid. You pervert!'

'I have no recollection whatsoever of ever meeting you or asking you to do any work for me or offering to sell you one of my doll's houses. Please stop texting me.'

But the pièce de résistance came from Lisa. It read: 'I am not at all surprised that you went to see *Fifty Shades of Grey*. I have no interest in knowing that I have exactly the same bath as Christian Grey! My daughter is only fifteen years old! How you can have the gall to ask me for money when you apparently listened to her having sex with someone three years older than her and did nothing about it is quite frankly beyond me. You are an accessory to rape! I do not expect to hear from you ever again.' To my utter shame, I realised then that telling her in my text that her bath was in *Fifty Shades of Grey* wasn't perhaps the most sensible thing to have done in the circumstances, but I wasn't expecting that response.

Many people assume that plumbers and other trades-people will rip them off. Websites like Trustatrader.com and Rated People have sprung up promising to protect the public from cowboys, but it's a double-edged sword. Tradespeople are often ripped off themselves by their clients for a variety of reasons. I accept that my actions on these three jobs can be seen in many different ways. Sometimes, people's assumptions are grossly unfair, but there's nothing I can do about that. I just have to accept it, and move on. But the question remains: Am I the villain in my own story? Or not?

8

Gay Week

London is one of the most cosmopolitan cities in the world. So if you have a business like mine, which relies solely on word of mouth, it is more or less inevitable that you will come into contact with a variety of people from very different parts of society. In many ways, that is the best part of my job. Eccentrics are the most fun to work for; and gay eccentrics are the best. I don't quite know how it happens, but, every now and then, I have a flurry of activity from within certain subcultures. I do a job for someone who is part of that subculture, they like me, and are happy with my work, so they tell their friends and, suddenly, I'm inundated with enquiries. That is what happened in what I now refer to as Gay Week.

Before I go any further, I hate people who say, 'I'm not homophobic, some of my best friends are gay,' when you know that it isn't true. So I'm going to come clean. I do not, as far as I know, have any gay friends, but I want to make it absolutely clear that this does not mean I am in any way homophobic. My son is gay and I love him to pieces. I wish I had gay friends. I really don't know why I don't. My daughter will testify that I have spent years jokingly encouraging her to be gay, which drives her mad, because, as I keep telling her, 'Being heterosexual is just so dull.' Unfortunately, it hasn't worked; *both* my children are looking for Mr Right. But I assure you, it wasn't for the want of trying. I had a theory that my lack of gay friends was actually something to do with a prejudice that existed within the gay community. I thought that because I was a plumber, a lot of gay people presumed I was homophobic, because it has a rather blokey, not very open-minded image. So I always do my best to disprove that.

It all started in the early summer of 2012. The build-up to the London Olympics was underway, and pink cherry blossom floated in the breeze and carpeted the footpaths and pavements with confetti. The golden rain of laburnum hung in front gardens, Boris Johnson was about to get stuck on a zip wire, and it was really starting to warm up when I received a call from a flat in Archway. It was Michelle, and she had a leak from her cold-water tank. Work was quiet at the time, so I went straight over. When I arrived, I thought twice about doing the job. Michelle's flat was in a run-down ex-council block at the back of an estate. It looked like it was full of crack dens. I was hesitant even to get out of my van. There were lots of kids wearing hoodies hanging around, who looked very much like they were dealing drugs. There was no lift in the block, so the only access to the top floor, where the flat was, was via a dimly lit concrete staircase that stank of urine and was littered with needles and other discarded rubbish. I was sure that if I left my van, someone would break into it and steal my tools, so I called Michelle and told her about my concerns. 'You're quite right. The kids round here are terrible,' she said, 'I'll come down and show you where to park.'

A few minutes later, Michelle appeared wearing full make-up, a long, blond wig, high heels, a short skirt and the most flamboyant multi-coloured shirt. 'Are you Nick?' she said, opening the passenger door and delicately stepping in.

'Yes,' I replied.

'Pleased to meet you. I'm Michelle. I'll show you where to go. You're quite right, it's far too dangerous to park it here.' She directed me to a road just round the corner. 'There's a police station at the end,' she said, closing the door behind her. 'It will be fine here. Even the crack addicts stay away from this road.' It was a pleasant street with a wide pavement. The houses were Victorian and most of them still had their original stained glass in the windows of their front doors. The front gardens were all well tended and filled with the buzzing of industrious bees. Michelle was very good-looking. I wouldn't have suspected she was a man if it hadn't been for the size of her hands and her Adam's apple. That rather gave it away. I took my tool-box out of the back of my van, locked it and put a padlock on the back. I trailed after her as she strode round the corner and into the estate. I couldn't help but check her out as she walked in front of me. Curiosity just got the better of me. 'Thank you so much for coming,' she said, turning round and catching me eyeing her up. 'No problem,' I said, 'You caught me at a good time. I'm about to go on holiday so I'm only taking on small jobs.'

'Oh, really? Where are you going?'

'The Dordogne. It's my wife's birthday, so we've rented a house with some friends.'

'It must be a big place.'

'Yes, it is. It's either going to be great or it's going to be a disaster. One or the other.'

'How long are you going for?'

'Two weeks.'

'That's a long time.'

'We're thinking of letting our flat out while we're away,' I told her. 'A client of mine just rented his house out to someone coming for the Olympics and he's gone to San Francisco for a month on the proceeds.'

'Wow. Now that sounds like fun,' she said, showing me up the stairs. As I entered that closed concrete staircase, the dulcet tones of nature were soon drowned out by the incessant thump of drum and bass, which slowly deadened my senses. When we got to the top, the music got louder and, as we walked down the open corridor towards her flat, it became almost unbearable.

'It's the one at the end,' she explained. 'My neighbour's a DJ in a club in Dalston.' Outside Michelle's front door was a pretty pastel-blue bench and lots of hand-painted plant pots. There were geraniums, foxgloves, delphiniums, daisies and French marigolds all lined up like they were queuing outside a nightclub. 'Pretty,' I said, putting my tool-box down.

'Thank you, I like it. It brightens it up a bit,' she said, opening the front door as the deep bass vibrations rattled the radiators. Inside, directly opposite the front door, was a picture of two policemen kissing. 'Come in,' she said, 'Do you like it? I do. There's something about it. The idea of gay policemen appeals to me.'

'Do you know any policemen who are gay?' I asked.

'No. That's why I like it. It's like a vision of the future. Like Martin Luther King – "I have a dream … ,"' she said, imitating Martin Luther King's voice.

'… that my four little children will one day live in a nation where they will not be judged by their sexual preferences but by their character …,' I continued, in the same accent.

'Exactly,' she said, laughing. She showed me into her bedroom, opened a built-in wardrobe, which was full of the most fabulous dresses, and pointed at the large watermark on the ceiling. 'Above here is the communal water tank. It feeds the whole block. I think it must be leaking.'

'Can I get access?'

'Yes, there's a loft hatch over there. It's a bit tight, but if you crawl along you'll see the tank.'

'Okay, leave it to me,' I said.

'Can I get you anything? Cup of tea?'

'No, I'm fine, thanks. If I have any more caffeine today, I'll start shaking.'

Fifteen minutes later, I had fixed the leak.

'It's all done,' I said, walking back down the stairs, carrying my tool-box.

'That was quick.'

'The arm on the ballcock had come loose and got twisted.'

'Sounds painful,' she said, smirking at me.

I laughed. 'It wasn't turning on and off properly.'

'Oh, I see. So was it overflowing?'

'A bit. Because it was twisted, it wasn't stopping the flow as it should.'

'I know how that feels.'

I laughed, 'Anyway …'

'Are you okay?' she asked. 'You're covered in cobwebs. Do you want a towel to wipe them off?'

'Thank you, that would be great.'

'So, how much do I owe you?'

'Just call it £35. It only took me fifteen minutes. I usually charge £70 for a call-out, but since I did it so quickly, let's say £35.'

'Are you sure? I don't mind paying you £70. I wouldn't have had a clue.'

'No, £35 is fine.'

'Fair enough. Thank you,' she said, handing me the money.

As I walked down the open corridor, the pungent smell of strong weed spiralled up the staircase, permeating all the floors. As I walked down towards the source, I was transported back to breakfast on Brighton Beach while I was at uni. The clubs were closing and crowds of young people headed down to the beach. It was midsummer and the cafés opened early to catch the clubbers before they went home. Ambient anthems filled the air. There must have been 500 people on the beach that morning, all smoking copious amounts of weed, drinking fruit smoothies, trying to replenish the vitamins they'd lost the night before, as the sun came up over the English Channel.

There were three kids at the bottom of those concrete steps. They had a deadness in their eyes and looked as if they'd just had a lobotomy. I was no stranger to self-destruction, but as I walked past them I was frightened. I no longer felt comfortable. I realised that I was drifting into the abyss of middle age, worrying about my future, out of touch with modern music and judgemental about the drugs that the kids of today were taking. I heard myself saying, 'It wasn't like that in my day, all this genetically modified crap, what's wrong with a bit of Thai,' but I didn't, I just minded my own business and walked briskly back to my van, worrying that I might get stabbed at any moment.

A few hours later I received a call from a man in Crouch End with a blocked basin. He lived in a flat overlooking Suicide Bridge (as it was known locally for obvious reasons). It wasn't the most desirable location. There was a parking warden at the end of the road. He was taking photos, writing down registrations and slipping tickets under windscreen wipers. I hovered around my van like the hummingbirds at the bird feeders that hung from my parents' balcony all those years ago in Mexico City. When the warden finally left, I knocked on the door. A tall middle-aged man with long hair, holding a piece of toast in a very flamboyant manner, flung the door wide open, wearing nothing but a thong. 'Ahhh, so you're the plumber! I've heard so much about you. Thank you so much for coming over. So prompt.'

'No problem.'

'Michelle tells me you're terribly good with your hands,' he said, stepping to one side to let me pass.

'Did she?'

'Yes. She said you were very quick. You don't hang about. You like to get straight down to it.'

'I try.'

'Good. That's what we like to hear. It's through here. My boyfriend clogged it up. God knows what he put down it. I shudder to think.'

'Okay,' I said, taking out my plunger.

'What's that?' he said, admiring the three-foot-long piece of plastic I took out of the bag I was carrying.

'It's a power plunger.'

'Is it indeed?'

I put it over the plug hole and plunged it hard several times and cleared the blockage.

149

'That's amazing,' he said. 'Michelle told me you're going to France?'

'Yes, that's right.'

'Oh, I adore the French. I lived there for several years when I was a young man.'

'Really, whereabouts?'

'Paris, of course!'

'Fabulous city, Paris.' I put the plunger away and followed him into his sitting room.

'Can I offer you anything? I didn't expect you to do it so fast. A piece of toast perhaps?'

'No, I'm fine thank you.'

'So how much do I owe you?' he said, walking across the room.

'Call it £35. The same as I charged Michelle.'

'She said you were very reasonable, here you are,' he said, handing me forty pounds. 'Keep the change. You should come down to The Glory sometime, you'd get loads of work.'

'Really, where's that?'

'What! You've never been to The Glory? Oh, it's out of this world. You must come down. You'll love it.'

'I'll have to check it out,' I said, taking the money.

* * * *

Later that afternoon, I got a call from a young man called Francesco. He lived in a one-bedroom flat with the most amazing view over London. His bath tap had broken, so I went straight round. When I got there, he opened the door and invited me in. It was clear that Francesco was gay. He was wearing very short shorts, a crop top that showed off his belly-button and big, chunky boots. He had delicate features and an array of facial piercings.

'The bathroom is straight through,' he said. He had, without doubt, the most effeminate voice I had ever heard. It was almost a caricature of itself. I couldn't actually believe it was his real voice. I thought he was putting it on. But he wasn't. He really did speak like that. Francesco was absolutely hilarious. He showed me into his bathroom and then he left. But over the course of the next hour, he kept appearing in the doorway and then he'd linger for a while. 'Would you like a biscuit?' he would say, if I turned round, or, 'Can I pass you anything?' or, 'Would you like me to hold it?' But the crowning moment was when I was bending over the bath and he quietly came in and stood behind me. I don't know how long he was there, because the top part of the tap had seized and I was struggling to get it to move. 'Is it tight?' he whispered in my ear. I almost jumped out of my skin. 'Yes,' I said, laughing. 'I'm just trying to get it to release.'

'Really,' he said, coyly. Two minutes later he took off his crop top, put on some music and came shuffling back into the bathroom. 'Do you like my music?' he said, wiggling his arse in front of me. 'They are my favourite band.'

'Who is it?' I asked.

'Boys II Men,' he replied, just as the tap's upper casing released. I unscrewed it and changed the washer.

'Oh, what a shame,' he said, as I put my tools away, 'We were just getting to know each other.'

Francesco was renting, I later found out, in more ways than one, so I didn't need him to pay me. His landlord would cover the cost. So, I politely shook him by the hand and left, while he was getting changed again, into God knows what.

The next day, I got a call from a barrister in Islington. It was a beautiful day. It looked as if the whole of London had been rendered in Technicolor. I drove straight to the barrister's house and knocked on his door. He couldn't have been more different from my previous client. He was posh, middle-aged and wearing a pin-striped suit. 'Oh thank you so much for coming,' he said, handing me a parking permit. 'The bloody thing's driving my mad.'

'What's the problem?' I asked.

'Our waste disposal won't stop whirring!'

He showed me through to his very elegant Poggenpohl kitchen with its floor-to-ceiling glass doors that opened up onto a colourful courtyard filled with exotic plants. The kitchen sink was near the window and the waste disposal was clearly jammed. 'I don't even know where the switch is,' he said.

'It's under here,' I said, turning it off.

'Oh, thank God for that.'

'You've got a choice,' I said, looking at it. 'I can take it apart and try to fix it, but if it's damaged, you'll need to get someone from the waste-disposal company to come and fix it; or I could take it out altogether. I'm not much of a fan of these. All they do is cause pipes to get blocked. You're far better off recycling your food waste. By shoving it down the drains, you're just feeding the rats and encouraging them to come closer to your house.'

'I hadn't thought of it like that. But I agree, take it out.'

An hour later, another very good-looking and very well-dressed man walked into the kitchen and offered me a cup of tea. 'I 'ear you're doing the rounds?' he said, with a slight French accent. I looked at him, slightly perplexed.

'You're mining the pink pound!' he said, laughing.

'Come to think of it, I have had quite a lot of calls from the LGBTQ community this week,' I replied. 'Far more than normal.'

'You're being recommended on Grindr.'

'Grindr? What's that?'

'It's a gay website. It's a dating site, really, but you can use it to recommend people too.'

'I had no idea. Where in France are you from?'

'A little town in the south-west.'

'I'm going next week. Whereabouts?'

'It's a pretty market town, not far from Bergerac.'

'I'm going to Domme.'

'Ah, Domme is gorgeous. It's a medieval village set on top of a hill overlooking the river. You'll love it. I'm from a place called Sarlat. It's about half an hour north of there. It's the largest town in the region, but it wasn't big enough for me.'

'Is that why you're here?'

'It's a long story.'

Just then, my phone rang. 'Excuse me,' I said, answering my phone.

'Hi, my name is Marcel. You come highly recommended. I have a rental flat. The tenant isn't there, because there's been an emergency. He's left the shower on because he couldn't turn it off. I need someone to go round and fix it as soon as possible.'

'Where is it?'

'Just behind Sainsbury's in Islington.'

'As it happens, I'm not that far away from there. Give me ten minutes and I'll see you there?'

'Can you come and pick the keys up from me and then let yourself in? I only live round the corner?' he said, without giving me a chance to speak.

Ten minutes later, I pulled up outside his house on Liverpool Road and a tall, very handsome man came out and gave me the keys. 'Turn right just before Sainsbury's and then follow it to the end and it's right there, next to the police station. I'll text you the address. Just ring me when you've fixed it. I'll text you the tenant's number now, probably best to let him know you're on your way round. Thank you so much, I really appreciate it.'

'Okay,' I said, taking the keys. Five minutes later, I arrived outside the flat and called the tenant's number. The phone rang until the answerphone kicked in. 'Hi. This is Jules. I can't get to the phone right now. If it's an emergency, do not wait for me to call you back, just go straight to A&E.' Beep ... I didn't quite know what to say to that so I opted for: 'Hi. This is Nick, the plumber. I'm just outside your flat. I understand your shower is broken. I've got the keys off your landlord, so I was just ringing to let you know I'm going to go in and try to fix it. I'll speak to you later.'

I opened the front door and stood there, staring at what was in front of me. I could hardly believe my eyes. Every inch of every wall was covered in cocks. Pictures of the male member were everywhere. Every shape and size was accounted for: erect, flaccid, black, white, big, little, pierced, tattooed. They were all there and, in case two dimensions weren't enough, there were plenty of three-dimensional examples perched on bookshelves. It was dildo art on a grand scale. He even had a fridge magnet the exact size and shape of a willy. Underneath it was a small piece of paper. It read, 'Shut the fridge and watch it wobble. This little rubber chode is the perfect gift that'll get a smile. Uncut and naturally shrivelled, the design is wonderfully inoffensive, leave notes for yourself or your loved ones with this perfect little willy magnet.' I couldn't believe it. I'd stumbled into a castle of cocks. Even the hands on the cuckoo-clock were penises and the pendulum was a set of balls. There were cacti everywhere in the bathroom, all standing firmly to attention. The pictures in the bathroom depicted scenes of men sitting on other men. Above the toilet, there was a picture of several naked men standing in a circle, with another naked man kneeling down in the middle. It was like nothing I had ever seen before. I felt like I'd accidentally walked onto a gay porn set. But I suppose even gay porn sets need to have working showers. So I got on with the job. After about an hour, I had managed to isolate the shower. I called the tenant, but there was still no answer. So I called the owner and explained that I had to order a part.

'He won't like it, but he'll just have to make do with baths,' said the owner. 'Don't worry, I'll tell him.'

I walked out of there like I was walking out of a sex shop, embarrassed, trying to get away before anyone saw me. I didn't mention anything about the decor in the flat to his landlord. I didn't think it was any of his business. But two days later, the part arrived and I called the tenant and arranged a time to go round. As it turned out, I was completely wrong, it wasn't a gay porn set at all. It was just a flat that was owned by a gay guy, who rented it to another gay guy, who was by his own admission, 'perhaps a little overly obsessed with cocks'.

If I'm totally honest, I was actually a little bit frightened to go back on my own. I almost called Ryan, just so I had someone with me. I suppose that does imply that I do have a degree of prejudice in me, but I think I was entitled to that, given his unusual taste in artworks and bric-a-brac. But I didn't call Ryan and I'm pleased I didn't, because he would have been hopeless, and I would probably never have worked for another gay person ever again. And I would have hated that. I went on my own. And when I got there, I realised just how stupid and ridiculous I had been. He wasn't anything like what I had imagined. He was a small, bald guy, with piercing blue eyes, who loved his mum and spent every penny he had going to the theatre. He was a lovely guy and I really liked him. He worked as a psychotherapist and specialised in helping middle-aged, suicidal gay men. That was why he had such an unusual message on his phone. After I fixed his shower, he came into the bathroom with a camera and said, 'Would you mind if I took a photo of your cock? It's for my montage?' I laughed and said, 'No. I think you've got enough.'

'Please yourself,' he said, walking out of the room. 'I usually do,' I replied, and he laughed and that was it. A few months later, I heard he went back to America and the owner sold the flat, but I'll never forget that montage of members, which he had hanging in his hallway, because now I know they were all real. He put them together himself and displayed them in pride of place opposite the front door in that Palace of Penises, which happened to be next door to one of the biggest police stations in North London.

I'm ashamed to say I still haven't been to The Glory. But, as it happens, our next-door neighbours also have a gay son and he works at The Glory, so I have a feeling my son is going to go, and if he does, so will we. You never know, I might actually crack it and manage to make myself a gay friend!

9

Cornwall Road

Several years ago, Jo and I went through a phase of watching lots of TV programmes about serial killers. It started with a programme called *Making a Murderer*, then we watched *The Ted Bundy Tapes* and it just spiralled from there. For three months, all we watched were programmes about psychopaths. Around this time, one of the properties I looked after was a basement flat in Bethnal Green, which was being rented to a very confrontational South African writer, who happened to write horror novels. He rented the flat with his much younger South American girlfriend, whose tongue was split at the end like a snake – I'd never seen anything like it before. She was also covered in tattoos and piercings. After they moved in, they asked if they could redecorate. The owner agreed. They took the bulbs out of all the overhead lights, painted the whole flat black and put black-out blinds over all the windows. The flat was full of skulls, black candles and other obscure objects and artefacts of the sort that might be used in satanic rituals. Above their bed, they painted a small, upside-down red cross. It looked like a portal to hell. Opposite the front door, they hung a grotesque, four-foot-square oil painting of a body with all the skin removed, so the muscles, tendons and ligaments were all exposed. He was writing a book about a serial killer who dabbled in the occult. I thought they were both strange, but I had no reason to think they would hurt anyone.

After they had been sharing the flat for nine months, the girlfriend called and told me they were splitting up and she was going to go back to South America, but he was going to stay on and pay the rent until he had finished his novel. Several months later, he called me in a complete state and told me that his girlfriend had died suddenly. I didn't want to question him about it, since he was clearly very upset, but when he told me that it was the girlfriend who I thought had moved out two months earlier, I started to become a little suspicious. Probably all those murder TV programmes I'd been binge watching affecting my judgement. I spoke to the landlord about it and we both agreed that despite it being odd, clearly something tragic had happened and it wasn't for us to interfere. A few days later, I went to see him and he appeared to be utterly devasted. He told me at that meeting that he had finished his novel and was not going to be renewing his lease, as he couldn't bear being in the flat where she'd died. I was shocked that she had actually died in the flat and I assumed that since she was only in her late twenties and she had clearly died suddenly, the police would naturally have been informed. So again, I did nothing. A couple of weeks later, he moved out and went back to South Africa, and I never heard from him again.

The day after he moved out, I received a call from someone in Finsbury Park. 'My toilet's broken,' he said, before I'd managed to say anything. 'Water's pissing out of it. Can you come and fix it?' he continued, still not allowing me to speak.

'I'm afraid I'm busy at the moment. Where are you?'

'Cornwall Road in Finsbury Park.'

'I might be able to get over to you later, is that any good?'

'What time?'

'Around six o'clock?'

'I've had to turn the water off. You can't come any sooner?'

'No, I'm afraid not.'

'Okay.'

'Text me your address and I promise I'll get over to you as soon as I can.'

It was just starting to get dark when I pulled up outside. The house was very run-down and clearly hadn't been touched for years. I came across a lot of places like that. I called Jo to let her know I was going to be late. She picked up the phone almost as soon as it started ringing.

'Hiyah. Anything all right?' I said, sarcastically.

'Ha ha, very funny. The kids are driving me crazy. Where the hell are you? I've got a business call in half an hour. I need you to take the kids out of the house.'

'Oh shit! I've just been called to another job. It's an emergency. He's had to turn the water off.'

'But you knew I had this call!'

'I'm sorry. Can't you take the kids round to your mum's?'

'It looks like I'm going to have to. That's really irritating. You know she'll give me a guilt trip.'

'I can't help it. I'm here now.'

'How long do you think you'll be?'

'I don't know. Hopefully not that long.'

'Okay, call me when you're done. Maybe you could pick them up from Mum's?'

'I'll do my best,' I said, ending the call.

As I approached the front door, the curtain twitched slightly in the front room. The windows were cracked, and the paint was peeling off. It looked like the whole place was slowly rotting from the inside out. 'Do you need a parking permit?' the man inside asked. I heard him shuffling around, but he still didn't open the door. Suddenly it opened just wide enough so he could pass the parking permit through the gap. He had powerful hands and long, dirty fingernails. I took the permit, scratched out the relevant time, walked back to my van and put it on the dashboard. Just then, my phone rang. It was Jo. 'Mum's out. I need you to come home right now. I can't talk to lawyers with the kids fighting.'

'I can't, he's already given me a parking permit. I'll be as quick as I can.'

Jo slammed the phone down. I thought about driving off and going to relieve Jo, but I didn't. If I drove off every time Jo needed me to look after the kids, I'd never do any work, I thought to myself. Anyway, we needed the money. So I grabbed my tool-box and walked back along the broken path. As I approached the front door, I heard him unfasten the chain. He opened the door slowly, but stayed behind it, as if he didn't want anyone to see him. I stepped inside and he quickly closed the door behind me. I turned to look at him. He was a tall, thin man, with greasy black hair, which he'd combed into a side parting. He was very pale and had expressionless, light-grey eyes. He stood with a slight stoop and was wearing thick black National Health-style glasses, black tracksuit bottoms and a black anorak, which didn't fit him properly and was ripped around the cuffs. 'I'm sorry about t' state of place,' he said in a very slow, deliberate way. At first I thought he was stoned, but he wasn't. There was just something creepy about him. His words slid into each other in a way that was unusual; they weren't pronounced individually, yet I got the feeling he'd chosen each one carefully before he said it. He had a strange accent, which I couldn't easily place. It was definitely Northern, but where up north I couldn't be absolutely sure. There was a slight Lancastrian twang to the way he enunciated the words, but my guess was that he came from somewhere in the Lake District. Somewhere remote. A farm miles away from anywhere, perhaps.

The house was stacked, floor to ceiling, full of crap. He had carved out a labyrinth of tunnels through it, just wide enough for one person to fit through. There were old rags hanging up at the windows, and dirty pans and plates piled high on every surface. He seemed anxious. He clearly didn't like me looking around. He pointed up the stairs, 'Tut toilet's up 'ere,' he said, fumbling with his keys and locking the front door behind me. 'There's no electric, it was cut off ages ago.'

'Are you squatting?' I said, taking my torch out of my tool-box.

'Aye, but don't worry, I got money to pay ye.'

I looked at him suspiciously and then slowly navigated my way up the stairs. Past an old lawn-mower, a set of bolt-cutters and an ancient-looking chainsaw without its chain. When I got to the top of the stairs, a rat ran across the landing and dived into a cupboard. There was an old axe leaning up against the wall. Its handle had split and the head was loose. 'I use it t' kill rats,' he said, seeing me look at it.

'It's in there,' he said, pointing to the cupboard. I turned and looked at him.

'You've got to be kidding me,' I said, pushing the door open slowly with my foot. I was half expecting the rat to jump out at me. I hate rats. I've always hated rats, ever since one jumped out of the plug hole when I was having a shower in Penang.

The smell was horrendous. I had to do everything I could to stop myself from retching. The toilet was full of shit. There was a dead rat in the centre of the floor with bluebottles buzzing around it. 'Jesus Christ!' I said, recoiling. I bumped into him. He stumbled back and put his hand out to stop himself from falling down the stairs. In doing so, he inadvertently pushed the bathroom door open. On the floor inside the bathroom was another dead rat and a small hatchet wrapped in a towel. 'Rats get everywhere,' he said, sitting down on a large cardboard box at the top of the stairs. I stepped back and peeked into the bathroom. There was a pentagram on the wall. In the far corner was an old cast-iron bath, which was chipped round the edges and looked as if it had blood stains round its rim. 'Cut meself earlier,' he said quickly, trying to regain his composure. He stood up and closed the bathroom door. As he got up off the cardboard box, I noticed the words 'One Shot' on the side of the box. I recognised it instantly. 'Is that One Shot?' I said, pointing at the box.

'Ay,' he said, nervously.

'That's 95 per cent sulphuric acid. It's powerful stuff. It'll burn your skin right off. You want to be careful with it,' I said.

'I am. I 'ad a blocked drain,' he said, nervously.

'You must have had a really bad blockage? There must be a dozen bottles of it in that box,' I said, stepping back and looking at him. He seemed very nervous now. As if I'd seen something I shouldn't have. But he didn't say anything.

'You need a new ballcock,' I told him. 'But that's the least of your problems. The rats have gnawed a hole in the pipe at the back of the toilet pan. They're basically coming straight up out of the sewers into your house. How long has it been like this?'

'It's been blocked for a while, but water only started pissing out of it this morning.'

'You need a new toilet. Trying to fix this is pointless.'

'I don't use it. I got 'nother one downstairs, but I've had t' turn water off so I can't use it,' he said, crossing his legs. 'I'm desperate for a piss,' he said, smiling. His teeth were nicotine-yellow. It looked like someone had painted them with a fluorescent yellow highlighter.

'If I disconnect the water to this one and turn the water back on, then you can use the one downstairs?'

'That would be great,' he said, still trying to hide the box of sulphuric acid.

'Okay, I'll need to get a cap out of my van, to close up the pipe.'

He turned around and I followed him back down the stairs to the front door, which he begrudgingly unlocked. When I got to my van, I opened the back, pretended to be looking for a cap, took out my mobile and pressed redial. Jo picked up straight away. 'Are you done?'

'No. I shouldn't be too long, though. Can you write down the following address?'

'Yes, why?'

I told her the address. 'It's a squat in Finsbury Park. It's where I'm working. It's fucking disgusting, full of rats.'

'Okay, I've written it down.'

'The guy's a bit freaky. There is a pentagram on the wall in his bathroom and he's got a box full of acid. I just thought you should know where I am.'

'What do you mean?'

'I don't know. I've probably been watching too many of those serial killer TV programmes.'

'Do you think he's dodgy?'

'I don't know. I just felt you should know where I was, that's all.'

'I can't take this right now. I'm about to have a conference call with a load of high-powered New York lawyers. I need you to come home and look after the kids.'

'Okay. I'm sorry. I just thought you should know where I am. That's all.'

'Okay, now you're really starting to freak me out.'

'It's just there was a hatchet in his bathroom, and it looked like there were bloodstains on the side of his bath.'

'Stop it. I can't take this! Where the hell are you? Are you still inside the house?'

'No. I'm outside. I've just gone to get a pushfit cap from my van.'

'Then leave! Get in your van and leave!'

'I can't. I've left my tools inside.'

'I don't care about your bloody tools. Get in your van and come home!'

'I'm not leaving my tools. Don't overreact, I just wanted you to know where I was that's all.'

'Don't tell me not to overreact. You can always buy new tools. What happens if he sinks an axe into the back of your head?'

'Funny you should say that. There's an axe outside the room I'm working in.'

'What!'

'Listen, I'm sure it's nothing. I just wanted you to know where I was. That's all. I've got to go.' I grabbed a cap and walked back towards the house.

'Who was that you were speaking to on't phone?' he said, slowly opening the front door, keeping back behind it so no one could see him from the street.

'Oh, it was just my wife. She was expecting me to come home, I just needed to tell her that I'd been delayed.'

I turned my torch back on and slowly made my way back up the stairs. I heard him lock the front door behind me and then follow me up. When I got to the landing, I took my pipe-slice out of my tool-box and opened the door to the cupboard. A rat jumped out from behind the toilet and brushed past my legs as it ran back down the stairs. 'Fuck off!' he said, trying to kick it as it ran past him. I pointed the torch into the cupboard to check there weren't any others, then stepped over the dead rat in the centre of the floor, cut the pipe feeding the cistern and pushed the cap onto it. 'There you go,' I said, relieved that another rat hadn't appeared from behind the toilet.

'Can you turn the water back on for me?' he asked. 'I sprained me wrist turning it off.'

'Sure, where's the stopcock?'

'In t' cellar,' he said. It was as if the words came out of his mouth in slow motion. They seemed to just hang there in the air for ages. They didn't, of course; I'm sure

I just imagined it, but it didn't matter, because from that moment on my heart started racing and my brain went into overdrive. I tried to conceal my fear, but I'm quite a transparent person and I suspect he picked up on it. I followed him back down the stairs towards the kitchen. Just as he was about to walk in, he turned and opened the door under the stairs and pointed down into the gloom. 'It's down there, at back, on right,' he said. There was an old rickety wooden staircase that led down to a cellar.

'Can't stand up down there, you'll 'ave to crawl on ye hands and knees,' he told me.

I looked down the stairs into the blackness. There was a terrible smell of defrosting frozen meat. Fortunately, at that very moment my torch flickered twice and then stopped working. 'It looks like the batteries have gone,' I said, relieved. 'I need to get my other torch out of my van.' I turned around and walked back towards the front door.

'I've got one,' he said, clearly not wanting me to go outside.

'No, it's all right. I want to get some WD40 as well. If it's stiff, a couple of squirts of that will loosen it up.'

I took my tools with me this time. I opened the back of my van, threw them inside, took out my phone and pressed redial. 'Have you left yet?' said Jo, picking up the phone.

'No. I'm just looking for some WD40. He's asked me to go down into his cellar to turn the water back on. I'm probably being paranoid, but he reminds me a bit of Dennis Nilsen!'

'That's it! I mean it, Nick. Get the fuck out of there! Leave! Leave right this minute. Don't you dare go back in there.'

'But he owes me fifty quid.'

'I don't care! It's not worth it! I'm not going to be widowed for fifty quid. He's clearly a madman. If you go back in there, you won't ever come back out. God knows how many people he's killed. I mean it!'

I hung up, grabbed the WD40 and walked back towards the house.

'Speaking to your wife again were ye?' he said, opening the door.

Just then my phone rang. 'You better not have gone back!' Jo was yelling down the phone. 'I'm being serious! Get the fuck out of there, right now!'

'Sorry, but I have to take this,' I said, walking back out of the front door.

'Can you stop being so melodramatic,' I whispered into the phone.

'If you go back in there, don't bother coming home. I can't live with someone who is constantly putting his life in danger! I can't take it. My nerves can't take it. COME HOME RIGHT NOW! GET INTO YOUR VAN AND COME HOME!'

I hung up and turned to him as he stood behind the door, keeping out of sight. 'I'm so sorry, I've got to go. I have an emergency at home. Here,' I said, giving him the WD40. 'Give it a couple of squirts with this, then leave it for ten minutes and you should be able to turn it back on yourself.'

'How much d' I owe ye?' he said, as I walked briskly towards my van.

'Don't worry about it, just call me when you're ready to change the toilet.'

I got into my van and drove off. When I got home, Jo was standing on the steps outside.

'I CAN'T BELIEVE YOU WENT BACK!' she said, throwing her arms up in despair as I walked towards her. 'HAVE YOU GONE COMPLETELY MAD? SOMETIMES I THINK YOU'VE GOT A DEATH WISH! I'M NOT READY TO BE ON MY OWN!'

'Calm down,' I said.

'WE'VE GOT TWO YOUNG CHILDREN! I CAN'T DO IT ON MY OWN!'

'I know.'

'It was a plumber who found human remains in the drains on Cranley Gardens! Don't ring me up and tell me you're working for someone who reminds you of Dennis Nilsen!'

'Sorry, but he did.'

'For God's sake! If you think someone's a mass murderer don't bloody work for them! I don't care how much you think we need the money! It's not worth it!'

'Okay, okay, stop having a go at me. I left, didn't I?'

'You shouldn't have gone back there in the first place!' she said, continuing to pace up and down. 'What would I do if you didn't come home? I never know where you are!'

'That's why I called you.'

'What did you expect me to think! You've never called me during a job before! Then suddenly, out of the blue, you call me and tell me you're working for someone who reminds you of Dennis Nilsen! Then you tell me to write down his address! The implication being, in case you don't come home! I've been beside myself with worry. I almost called the police!'

'To say what?'

'My husband is working for a serial killer in Finsbury Park,' she said, smiling at what she had just said.

'Well, I'm pleased you didn't,' I said, laughing as I put my arm around her.

'You need to be more careful,' she said, wrapping her arms around me.

'I didn't think you cared,' I said, facetiously.

'Of course, I care.'

'I think we should probably stop watching any more programmes about serial killers,' I said, laughing.

'I think you might be right, otherwise I'm going to think you've been buried under someone's patio every time you're late back from work!' she said with a smile.

10

A Woman Scorned

Once a year, I meet up with an old friend in central London. We have dinner, then we usually go for a walk. This year we went for some seriously posh nosh. It was a warm evening, so afterwards we sauntered down The Strand and wandered over Waterloo Bridge. Half-way across, we stopped. The whole of London was lit up. The National Theatre shone like a bright red ruby on the other side of the river, inviting us south. The heat of the day was starting to subside and a cool calmness was descending on the centre of the city. We strolled down the South Bank, soaking up the summer vibe. There was an old man playing the sombre tune 'St James Infirmary' on his saxophone. People were gathering on the wide promenade as a couple of acrobats were preparing to perform. One of them had a huge pile of books on his head. As we walked past, he shouted, 'I'm an accountant, I only do this to balance the books!' I laughed, and my friend threw some change into his hat. It occurred to me that he might actually be telling the truth. London is such an expensive place to live. Dinner in town will soon teach you that! For this reason, lots of Londoners have a side line to bring in a bit of extra cash.

Why shouldn't an accountant also be an acrobat? A little bit of this and a little bit of that, is a cockney expression after all. Nowadays, it implies a degree of dodginess, but surely not all side lines are shady?

'I've come across a few bizarre extra-curricular activities,' I said, as we approached the London Eye.

'Oh really, like what?' said my friend.

'I once did a job for a lady. She worked as the secretary to a famous singer in the seventies.'

'Who was it? Anyone I've heard of?'

'No, I don't remember his name, but she lived in one hell of a pad. It was a palatial porn palace in the poshest part of Paddington,' I said, as we wandered on towards Westminster Bridge. Suddenly, the summer of 2006 came flooding back to me as I recounted the tale of Sophie and her seriously strange side lines.

Ryan and I were installing a mixer tap in a medical centre in Maida Vale when Sophie first called me. She lived in a large house in Little Venice, which wasn't far from where we were working. So, after we were done at the doctors, we went straight round. I didn't typically introduce Ryan to people I hadn't met before. He tended to terrify them. It was the scar on his face. He looked like he'd been slashed with a sword, and people can be prejudiced against folks with facial flaws. So, I left him in the van, grabbed my plunger and walked up the stairs that led up to her front door. The Regent's Canal ran down the side of the road. It was full of barges and houseboats: a fellowship of floating families, all trying to live cheaply in the heart of central London. A few long-haired men were beginning to stir. Old-fashioned kettles were whistling, and the seductive smell of freshly ground coffee was escaping the portholes and flowing down the pavement. Summer had finally arrived. I figured I'd fix her toilet in a few minutes, then we'd be on our way. She answered the door in a cheerful, multicoloured dressing gown. In the bright sunshine she looked as if she was wearing Joseph's amazing Technicolor dreamcoat, a divine apparition from a bygone era. Ryan and I had started early that day to beat the traffic. Our next job wasn't for another hour, so I had plenty of time, and she looked like an interesting person to talk to.

'That was quick,' she said, tying her hair into a ponytail. She had been a model in the seventies and, although she was about to turn sixty, she looked more like thirty-five. She was tall, long-limbed and blonde. Her hair colour wasn't natural and, as I was soon to find out, not much else was either. The first thing I noticed were her eyes. She had the most piercing pale-blue eyes; they were almost grey, and she never seemed to blink. Her complexion was perfect; there were no laughter lines, nor crow's feet – her skin was stretched tightly across her cheeks. She had the appearance of a china doll, not least in that there was no movement in her face. She seemed to have only one expression: complete and utter surprise, which made her very hard to read. Her house was like an eighties porn palace. It had white marble floors throughout, a sunken lounge, full of white leather furniture, and a wide staircase that led up to a minstrels' gallery. It was like something out of the film *Scarface*. At any moment Al Pacino might appear, carrying a submachine gun.

'I got your number off a friend of mine,' she said, showing me up the stairs. 'She's been raving about you.'

'That's nice. Who's your friend?'

'Rebecca Robson. She lives up near Jack Straw's Castle,' she replied, marching up the stairs.

'I remember Rebecca. Her husband played the piano. He drinks the same white wine as my wife.'

'Really? Which wine is that?'

'Vouvray. It's from the Loire Valley. She won't drink anything else. He's the same.'

'Really? I didn't know that. I'll have to get a bottle for when they next come around. The toilet's in my en suite. Please mind the mess. I wasn't expecting you so soon,' she said, walking across the minstrels' gallery and opening the door at the far end. In the centre of her bedroom was a large, pink waterbed with two mirrored chrome side tables. There was an open drinks cabinet, full of empty bottles of vodka, and mirrors across the back wall. The rest of the room was covered in black-and-white palm-tree wallpaper. It looked like the boudoir of a Colombian cocaine baron from the decade that fashion forgot.

'The toilet's through there,' she said, trying to distract me from staring at all the empty bottles of booze. The bathroom was quite something; it had clearly been done in the early eighties. I'd never seen anything like it. The whole room was clad entirely in pink marble. It had a huge pink jacuzzi with gold taps shaped like a swan. The bath could easily accommodate at least four people lying side by side. The ceiling was mirrored, so you could lie in the bath and admire yourself (or more likely, whoever happened to be on top of you at the time). 'The toilet's through there,' she said, pointing to a secret door. 'Just push it. The handle's on the inside.'

I could hear a whirring sound as soon as I opened the door. 'It's the Saniflo,' I said straight away, kneeling down to look at it.

'Not again! I bet my cleaning lady flushed a tampon down it this morning.'

'That'll do it. The string gets wrapped around the motor.'

'I can't believe it! I only changed it a few months ago. It cost me a thousand pounds.'

'Yes, it would. They aren't cheap and this one's built in. I'm going to have to dismantle the whole room to change it.'

'Can you change it for a normal toilet?' she said, looking at me intently. I got the feeling she'd asked that question before. And a normal toilet couldn't be fitted in that location without a massive amount of work.

People have always fascinated me, so I naturally always ask lots of questions. As a plumber, you have to, because you can't fix a fault unless you first find out what's causing it. Plumbers are essentially domestic doctors. They pinpoint problems, then they suggest solutions. There are usually several solutions to any particular problem. Picking the right one depends on the person. Most people don't know what they want until I present them with some options. But that wasn't the case with Sophie. She knew exactly what she wanted. I thought she wanted me to fix her toilet, but as she continued to talk to me, it was clear that what she actually wanted was for me to build her two new bathrooms, convert her husband's study into a consultancy room and turn her box room into an office. Sophie was looking to shake her life up and, thanks to her friend Rebecca Robson, she'd already decided that I was the person she wanted to help her do it.

Ryan was really riled when I finally got back in the van.

'Where the fuck have you been?' he said, as I put the key in the ignition.

'Sorry, I was just talking to her about all her options,' I said, pulling out.

'I've been sitting here, scratching my arse, for over an hour. What do you mean, options! She's got a blocked bog. How many options has she got?'

'Lots.'

'Did you fix it?'

'No, she's going to think about it and then get back to me.'

Ryan clearly wasn't going to let it lie. He looked like he was about to explode. It was roasting in the van and stale Guinness was escaping from every one of his pores.

'What's up with you?' I said, turning to look at him.

'You took the keys. I couldn't open the window. What were you talking to her about?'

'Her husband, a bit about her clematis and her upcoming holiday to Hawaii.' I knew it drove Ryan mad the way I talked to my clients. Ryan only talked about practical things. He never asked questions, because he didn't want anyone to ask him any. This only strengthened my suspicions that he had something to hide. *The trouble with being a terrorist is that you're afraid to talk*, I thought to myself as I drove off.

'Really,' he said. I could almost see the steam coming out of his ears. 'That sounds fascinating. What's that got to do with fixing her fucking toilet?'

'It's got everything to do with it.'

'How does talking to her about a clematis help fix a toilet? What even is a clematis?'

'It's a climbing plant.'

'I thought it was a sexually transmitted disease!'

'No, that's chlamydia.'

'What's that got to do with a blocked bog?'

'Do you want to know?'

'Yeah, I really want to know.'

'Okay, I'll tell you. Her toilet's blocked because her cleaning lady flushed a tampon down it.'

'So what?'

'It's a Saniflo.'

'What's that got to do with a climbing plant?'

'She asked me to come up with a permanent solution, so it never happens again.'

'That's easy. Don't flush a tampon down it.'

'I said that, but she wants to change it for a normal toilet. The only way to do that would be to remodel the bathroom and run a new soil stack up the front of her house. But there's a clematis growing right where the new soil stack would have to go. So, I suggested I replant it once I'd installed the new pipe. Basically, she wants me to renovate her whole house while she's away on holiday in Hawaii.'

'Fair enough,' he said, licking his Rizla. I could see the cogs turning in Ryan's brain as he thought about another way to frame his frustration. After five minutes, he threw his fag out of the window and said, 'How did you get from fixing her bog to renovating her whole bloody house?'

'I asked her lots of questions about her life, while I was simultaneously talking to her about her plumbing problems. For example, I know that she's in the process of splitting up from her husband. I know that he's a bit of a prick and has been playing away from home with his personal trainer. I also know he wants to move to Monaco. So, reading between the lines, she needs her house to start making her some money. She wants to turn her box room into an office, because she's setting up a new model agency for mature models from the seventies and eighties. Then, she wants me to convert her husband's old study into a new consultancy room. It's going to have a day bed in it with a light over the top of it and a strange dental unit with a fridge and sink in it. Christ knows what she's going to use that for, but she's clearly got an idea. Then she wants me to transform one of the bedrooms on the top floor into another bathroom, to create a "special guest suite", whatever that is. To do that we'll have to run a new soil stack up the front of the house. So, she might as well remodel her other bathroom at the same time. That way we can get rid of her tampon toilet and replace it with a normal one. That's why she needs some time to think about it.'

Ryan shut up and started looking at his phone.

That night, I sat down to do Sophie's quote. 'You know it never ceases to amaze me what can come from going to fix a broken bog,' I said, closing my computer. Jo was already in bed reading a book about the benefits of cranial therapy.

'Especially when she's got an axe to grind and her husband's minted,' Jo commented. 'You have to be a millionaire to move to Monaco,' she said, folding the page over and turning off the light.

Two days later Sophie called me in a bit of a state. 'I need to talk to you about the plans, can you come over?' It was an order not a question.

'I'm sorry, I'm busy today, but I can come over first thing tomorrow morning. How about 7 a.m.?'

'Okay, see you then,' she said, slamming the phone down.

When I got there, she was standing in the doorway. 'My husband's moved out,' she said, closing the door behind me. She'd clearly been crying, but she was still quite composed. Her pupils were dilated, and she was talking manically. It was like her brain was moving too fast for her mouth. 'We've come to an arrangement. I'm keeping the house. He's going to cover the maintenance. I want you to do everything we discussed. But I want him to pay for it. I've told him the only way to fix the toilet is to remodel the whole bathroom and he's agreed to cover that. He's also agreed to convert the box room into an office and his old study into my new consultancy room. I haven't told him about anything upstairs. It's complicated.'

'Okay. I don't care. So basically, you want me to secretly build you an extra bathroom and get your husband to pay me for it?'

'Exactly.'

'Okay, it's no skin off my nose, as long as he pays me.'

'Don't worry. He'll pay you and, if he doesn't, I'll pay you myself. Do we have a deal?' she said, holding out her hand.

'When do you want me to start?' I said, taking her hand. She was a nervous wreck. On the outside, she was calm, but inside, she was shaking. I could feel it through her fingers.

'I want you to do it while we're in Hawaii,' she said, quickly letting go of my hand. 'My husband's coming with me, then he's flying down to the south of France for a few weeks, so by the time he's back it needs to be finished. Do you think that's doable?'

'Anything's doable if you throw enough money at it.'

'Good. Send me the quote again. Keep the price the same. Take out any mention of building another bathroom on the top floor and I'll get him to agree to it.'

That evening, after dinner, I sat down to change the quote. 'There's something strange about this woman. I don't know what it is, but she makes me nervous,' I said, making the amendments.

'Well, don't do it if you think it's going to be a nightmare,' said Jo, pouring herself a glass of Vouvray.

'No, it's not that. She's very highly strung, but I think I can handle her.'

'You've had enough practice,' said Jo, smiling.

I laughed. 'It's the situation. I haven't even met her husband and yet he's supposed to be paying me,' I said, pressing send.

'As long as he pays you, who cares?' said Jo, taking a sip of her wine.

'That's true, but I'd like to at least meet him.'

Just then, my phone rang. It was Sophie. 'I just thought I'd let you know that my husband's approved the quote,' she said, without leaving any time for me to reply. 'My first guest is arriving in five weeks, so the top floor needs to be finished by the 5th of August. My husband's just transferred half the money, he'll pay the rest at the end.'

'Okay,' I replied, slightly stunned by the machine-gun burst of information I was being hit with down the phone. 'I'll get everything set up then.'

'Good. See you on Monday. We're leaving for the airport at 9, so be here for 7.30, I want to go through everything before we leave.'

'Okay.'

The line went dead.

'I'm telling you, there's something not right,' I said to Jo, feeling worried. 'Mind you, he's just paid me for half the job, and I haven't even started it yet.'

The next day, I primed the Misfits. Everyone was available. The only problem was that Chris's daughter was about to give birth, so he couldn't commit to the full five weeks. But I convinced him to do it anyway, on the understanding that I'd find someone else if need be. Little did I know what I'd let myself in for. I gave everyone the address and agreed to meet them there at 8.30 a.m. That way I could have an hour with Sophie before they arrived. Chris picked up Ryan, who couldn't drive. He'd never been sober long enough to learn. Fi brought Big Pete, because he'd just lost his licence for drink-driving through Dalston. Chris and Ryan were late because Chris had had to stop at Jewson's to buy a new jigsaw. He already had ten jigsaws. Chris was addicted to buying power tools, particularly when he was anxious. He couldn't pass a tool shop without buying something. It was a real problem. Chris had more power tools than all the rest of us put together. He lived in a tiny flat in Tottenham, with no central heating, but he had more power tools than a main contractor. Some of the Misfits drank, others took drugs; Chris was permanently purchasing power tools. Something told me I was in for a rocky ride.

Sophie was already packed when I arrived. 'I hope you don't mind me asking, but why are you going on holiday with your husband if you've just split up?' I said.

'We booked it before and it's not refundable. We're going to Hawaii and he's paying. I wasn't going to miss out on that! Anyway, I want him out of the way while you're doing the work.'

'Hell hath no fury ...'

'You have no idea,' she said, laughing. 'The bathroom on the top floor needs to work for someone who's just had surgery,' she said, closing the door so no one else could hear.

'I don't know what that means,' I replied.

'I want you to obscure all the windows. I've bought some film to stick on the glass. It's over there. It's extremely important that no one can see in. The shower needs to be easily accessible. It has to be big enough so I can get in with them. My guests will need help washing when they first arrive. There needs to be a fold-down seat in the shower so they can sit down. The showerhead must be movable, so it can be pointed away from any vulnerable areas. I've ordered a sink to go over here like the ones you get in hairdressers, with a reclining barber's chair to go in front of it, so they can lean back while I wash their hair without any water touching their face. The vanity unit needs to be plumbed in over here, which they can use to brush their teeth and to provide them with enough storage for all the oils and creams that they are going to need. The basin is big enough so they can wash in it if the shower is just too painful. As I said, my first guest arrives in four weeks. The day after I get back. She's coming from Switzerland, so it has to be finished by then.'

I didn't quite know what to say, so I just nodded.

'Good. Any problems, just email me. Make sure you buy the best of everything and send me pictures of what you propose. Honolulu's eleven hours behind, so, if you need to talk to me, call first thing in the morning or last thing at night. I presume you've got the money,' she said, handing me the keys. 'I can't wait to see it when I get back,' she said, smiling, as her husband pulled up in his Porsche. He opened the trunk, she put her suitcase in, and they sped off.

'This place is un-bloody-believable,' said Big Pete, walking into the kitchen. 'It's an eighties nightmare!' He was right. The cupboards were bright orange and the worktop was avocado-coloured. The floor was tiled in bright green hexagonal tiles and it had light-blue lights dangling from the ceiling. It looked like someone had vomited, and then decided to build a kitchen out of it. Ryan opened the sliding door and walked out onto the patio.

'I bet they used to have some great parties here back in the day. Where's the soil pipe?' he said, looking up at the house.

'I have no idea. Why don't you have a look around. I'll make some coffee. There's a swimming pool down at the end of the garden. You'll get a better view from down there,' I said, pressing the switch on the side of the kettle. As I watched them all walk across the lawn, my mind began to wander.

Suddenly, I had this daydream. I was surrounded by people with big hair and big glasses. 'Club Tropicana' was blasting out of the sound system in the sunken lounge. Young men were dancing around the pool in tight, white jeans, off-the-shoulder sweatshirts and espadrilles. Women, wearing big hats and ruffled white shirts with shoulder pads, were stretched out on the white, plastic sun loungers strategically placed around the pool. A couple of middle-aged Mediterranean men were trying to chat them up. At the far end of the pool was a very serious-looking Colombian businessman, who looked like Pablo Escobar. He was sipping a piña colada, surrounded by bodyguards wearing tight, black trousers, bright Hawaiian shirts and white, patent-leather ankle boots with Cuban heels. They looked like a dance troupe from the dangerous jungles of the Darién Gap. At the other end of the pool was a thatched cocktail bar, which had been lifted straight out of the Virgin Islands. Sitting at the bar was a young musician talking to his manager about how to break into the American music market. Two middle-aged men with enormous sideburns were discussing Aberdeen's defeat of Real Madrid in the 1983 European Cup Winners' Cup, while a group of TV execs were standing on the lawn talking about the death of Diana Dors and Rock Hudson's recent AIDS announcement. Robert Maxwell was talking to a bunch of back-benchers on the minstrels' gallery. Sophie was walking towards me with someone who looked like Peter Stringfellow. It was Melvin, her husband. He had the appearance of a barrow boy who'd become a banker and made a fortune in Thatcher's Britain. 'Club Tropicana' slowly faded out and 'Two Tribes' took its place. As the song started to build, the kettle began to boil and, as the song was about to reach its crescendo, the switch clicked and, just like that, I was transported back to 2006, making coffee for a group of balding builders so Sophie could set up some rather bizarre businesses inside her mansion in Maida Vale.

I walked down to the pool, carefully carrying four cups of coffee. Ryan and Big Pete were sitting at the bar trying to work out what Campari tasted like. Chris was half asleep on one of the sun loungers clutching his new jigsaw close to his chest. Fi was feeding the fish in the pond at the far end of the garden, sipping her Lapsang Souchong. 'Right,' I said, trying to create some momentum. 'Ryan, you disconnect everything in the bathroom upstairs. Chris, you start building the wardrobes in the bedroom on the top floor. Fi, I need you to check the fuse board, then put two new lights into what will be the consulting room and change all the lights on the top floor for dimmable LEDs. Big Pete, you come with me – we're going to dig a hole.'

The first setback came when I couldn't find the soil pipe. It ran down the back of the house, then came underneath it, went through the front garden and into the sewer, which ran down the road at the front. The new soil pipe was going to run down the front of the house and since there wasn't a manhole in the front garden we had to find it to connect the new soil pipe into it. Big Pete and I lost almost a stone each in two days. It was baking hot and we both must have sweated out twenty pints each day, the only difference was Big Pete drank them again that night. We dug three different holes before we finally found it – five feet underground.

Digging a hole that deep can be dangerous. The sides can collapse, which is what happened. Big Pete was four feet down when the earth on one side started to subside. Fortunately, he saw it moving and managed to jump out just before it caved in. Otherwise, I don't think I'd have been able to get him out. I'd never seen Big Pete move that fast. Twenty stone came flying out of the hole like an overweight Jack-in-the-Box on a bonfire. After that, he refused to dig any more. So, I had to dig the rest. I hate digging. When I eventually found the soil pipe, I carefully cleared the clay from around the pipe and told Big Pete to go and tell everyone not to use any water. As I finished cutting through the pipe, there was a sudden rush of water and I found myself knee-deep in Ryan's breakfast. He was apparently wearing ear defenders when Big Pete shouted up the stairs, though I suspect he did it because he found it funny. Unfortunately, there was so much clay, the water wouldn't dissipate, so I made Ryan bail it out. It was midday and almost a hundred degrees when he climbed down into that hole. He had to fill a bucket, then pass it above his head to Big Pete so he could tip it down the drain in the road. By the time he finished, he was completely covered in his own shit. He didn't find it so funny after that! No one ever said plumbing was a glamorous profession, but sometimes it's downright disgusting.

The next day, Chris's daughter went into labour. He was up a stepladder at the time. When he got the phone call he fainted, fell off his stepladder and broke his wrist. So, I had to take him to hospital (he was fine and over the moon that he'd become a granddad for the first time) but this meant I then had to find someone else at very short notice. The only person I knew would be available at the last minute was Jimmy. Jimmy was a very good joiner, but he had a profound personal-hygiene problem. I tried to talk to him about it, but it didn't make any difference. He couldn't help it. There was something seriously wrong with his sweat glands. But desperate times called for desperate measures. The next two weeks were swelteringly hot, and Jimmy was working in the hottest part of the house. By nine o'clock in the morning the smell of Jimmy's body odour was unbearable. You could smell him as soon as you walked into the house and he was three floors away. The next day Big Pete and Ryan both turned up to work wearing nose clips. They looked like a pair of overweight synchronised swimmers. After that, everything went to plan, until the day that Sophie was due to get back.

I'd given Jimmy the day off and I'd opened all the windows, but it was no good. The smell had permeated into every part of the building. So, I went to pick up some industrial air freshener. When I got back, I found Fi unconscious on the daybed in the consultancy room. She'd drilled into a live wire in the ceiling while she was up a ladder. The rubber soles on her Doc Martens probably saved her life. Fortunately, once she'd had a cup of camomile, she was fine. Then, I walked down the garden and found Big Pete swimming in the pool wearing nothing but his nose clip. 'What the fuck's going on?' I said, walking up to the edge of the pool. 'I finished filling the 'oles. It's so bloody 'ot, I thought I'd 'ave a quick dip,' he said, putting his hands on the side and heaving himself out. It was like watching an enormous white whale wearing nothing but a nose clip emerge from the depths and beach itself on the side of a bathing pool. 'Jesus! Put it away,' I said, as he turned around and plonked his enormous posterior on the edge of the pool. 'Have you got a towel?' he said, taking off his nose clip. Fortunately, his belly was so big, it hid his bits.

'I know it looks like a porn set, but this is ridiculous,' I said. 'I feel like I've walked onto the set of *Readers' Wives*! Put your pants on for Christ's sake, she'll be back any minute. Where's Ryan?'

'He's gone for a pint. I planted the clematis where you said. It's covered the new soil pipe. It's almost invisible,' he said, standing up to pull up the most enormous pair of pants I'd ever seen. They looked like a two-man tent.

Big Pete finished drip-drying, put his clothes on and was making a right mess of obscuring the windows, when Sophie arrived home. Fi was fully recovered and was finishing the lights in the consultancy room. Ryan was still in the pub – I'd told him not to come back. I was putting the finishing touches to the bathroom in the special guest suite.

Despite the palaver of the previous hour, I was really proud of what we'd achieved while Sophie was tanning herself in the tropics. Both bathrooms were among the best we'd ever built. They cost a small fortune. Everything was top of the range. It's not surprising that her husband lost it. He hadn't realised that my quote was just for the labour. I hadn't included any of the fixtures and fittings, because the prices vary so greatly. He'd flippantly told Sophie to choose whatever she wanted, thinking they were included, so she got me to buy the best of everything and it came to a tidy sum. Initially, I felt quite sorry for him, particularly when Sophie told me how much the holiday had cost, but that didn't last long. Sophie's husband was just as I'd imagined him. He was the epitome of everything that was wrong with being nouveau riche in the eighties. He was loud, brash, obnoxious and possibly the most revoltingly smug person I've ever met. So, it served him right; he shouldn't have shagged his personal trainer.

That night, Jo booked a holiday. It had been ages since we'd been away. She found a last-minute deal on a house in the Highlands. It wasn't exactly what we wanted, but beggars can't be choosers, so we booked it. I wanted sun, sea, sangria and lots of sex. What I got was miserable weather, midges, malt whisky and a week with my mother-in-law. And to make matters worse, the only availability was for the following week, so that meant I was going to have to work all hours to get everything finished before we went away.

Sophie had been over the moon with everything when we she got back. She threw her arms around me and kissed me on both cheeks. We still had to convert the box room, so we would be there for another week, but it felt good that she was happy with what we'd done. But the next day, she asked me to follow her up to the bathroom on the top floor. When I walked in there were Post-it notes stuck to some of the tiles.

'What's going on?' I said.

'They're slightly proud. The tiles. They're not even. It's not perfect. Feel it. You can't see it with the naked eye. But if you rub your hand over it, there's definitely a faint discrepancy.'

'Well, it's possible,' I said, rubbing my hand over a few, 'But, as you say, you can't see it.'

'It doesn't matter. It's there,' she said, blinking manically. I'd never seen her blink before and yet now she couldn't seem to stop.

'There's nothing I can do. I can't retile it. Your guest is about to arrive. I'm sure she won't even notice. I promise you, I was meticulous when I tiled it. It's almost impossible to get it absolutely perfect,' I said, peeling off the Post-it notes.

'Oh, she'll notice. She notices everything. That's why she's done what she's done. That's why she put herself through it,' she said, twitching and blinking without pause.

Just then, a Bentley with blacked-out windows pulled up outside. A woman stepped out, wearing a big hat and sunglasses. Sophie showed her straight up to her suite. I couldn't see who it was, because her face was bound in bandages. Sophie ignored me for the rest of the week, she was so preoccupied with looking after her guest. She basically became her private nurse. She made all her meals, assisted her in the bathroom and helped her to get dressed. From that point on, we weren't allowed upstairs and the guest never came out of her room, so I never saw her again. I've always wondered who was behind those bandages. A movie star, perhaps. Who knows? Whoever it was, Sophie treated her like royalty.

The next day, a steady stream of very well-dressed middle-aged women started to arrive at the house. They had a quick chat with Sophie, then they both disappeared into the new consulting room. They were in there for about half an hour, then they all came out wearing large hats and sunglasses. None of us could work out what was going on. Big Pete thought she must be dealing drugs. He reckoned the whole place was a front for a Colombian drug cartel. Ryan thought she was a spy, passing information to Putin. Fi thought she was a madam and all the women were high-class hookers. As the week went on, more and more women kept arriving. Friday was our last day and they were queuing up. Whatever it was Sophie was doing in there, lots of people wanted it!

It was almost eleven o'clock at night when I finally finished the job, so I arranged to pick up my tools the next day. Jo and I were due to leave to go on our holiday at 10 a.m. the following morning. Jo always found packing stressful, so picking up my tools was a great excuse to get me out of the house. At least then I'd be out of the firing line. I hated going on holiday straight after I finished a job. I spent the first few days sleeping and the rest of the time worrying that something was going to go wrong while I was away. Sophie had arranged for her husband to come over to settle up. My plan was to pick up my tools, get paid, pack the car and then drive non-stop to the north of Scotland. There was absolutely no margin for error. Any slippage would have massive repercussions for my marriage. Jo was extremely pedantic about leaving on time. She once hyperventilated because we were half an hour late getting to Heathrow. I'd promised her I'd be back by 9.30 a.m. So, when she called me at 9 to tell me she was ready, I knew I had to get a move on. I was very relieved when Sophie's husband finally pulled up in his Porsche.

'What do you think of the old house?' he said. He was wearing ripped designer jeans, white slip-on shoes and a white shirt that was open to his waist. He looked like Bill Bailey in the TV comedy *Black Books*, when he becomes a male prostitute for men with a fetish for beards. 'We had some great parties here. We knew everyone in the eighties – models, musicians, media moguls, you name it, they were all here. My name's Melvin by the way,' he said, holding out his hand. Every finger on his right hand had a gold ring on it. He had a thick gold chain around his wrist and another one round his neck. There was no doubt about it, Melvin looked like a total tosser. I could see why Sophie had decided to ditch him.

'Sophie tells me you've brought the old place into the twenty-first century. Always very efficient, our Soph. A real perfectionist. If she decides to do something, she always takes it to extremes. Never happy. That's why she had all those operations. If you look closely, when she's not wearing make-up, you can see the scars,' he said, watching me, waiting for me to respond. 'Don't tell me you haven't noticed. She's had so many facelifts, she can use her arse as a pillow,' he said, laughing. 'She tells me you've turned my old study into a Botox studio, whatever that is. She's setting up a model agency for mature models. I don't care. She can do what she likes. I'm out of here. I've just made a mint and I'm moving to Monaco. I'm sick of paying tax. It's a mug's game,' he said, walking up to the front door. 'Hello darling,' he said, kissing Sophie on both cheeks. 'I haven't seen you since we were in Hawaii.' Sophie smiled a fake smile and quickly closed the door behind him. 'So, what do you think of my wife's new tits?' he said, suddenly turning around to face me like a gun-slinger in the Wild West. I didn't know what to say in response to that, so I didn't say anything.

'Just kidding. They cost me a fortune,' he said, laughing. 'So I understand you want some more money?'

'That's right.'

'How much do you want?'

'£8,000. That's what was agreed.'

'Is that all?' he said, laughing, taking out a wad of £50 notes and throwing it to me. 'What's going on upstairs, Soph?'

'Nothing,' said Sophie, nervously.

'I heard you'd turned the top floor into a suite for people who've just had surgery.'

'Who told you that?'

'It doesn't matter who told me!' he said, walking towards the stairs.

'Okay, stop. Don't go up there,' she said. 'I promised her no one would go up there apart from me.'

'So, it's true.'

'So, what if it's true? It's my house.' Sophie said.

'I paid for it, though! Didn't I? I bet she got you to include it in my bill?' he said, staring at me like he'd just caught me with my hands in his safe.

'I'm sorry, but this really is none of my business,' I said.

'It *is* your business if I say it's your business!' he shouted. 'Now, let me ask you again. Did you include it in my bill?'

'I really have to go. I'm supposed to be driving to Scotland,' I said, putting the money in my man bag.

'There's only three grand there. I'm not paying for her to have any more fucking plastic surgery. That's why you built it, isn't it? So, you can employ someone to look after you when you have your next operation.'

'No. I did it to help other people,' she admitted. 'I know what it's like to have to stay in hospital till the swelling goes down. I want to offer people a sanctuary. Somewhere to recover. It's not for me. Honestly,' she said, begging him to calm down. Then she turned and looked at me. 'I'm so sorry about this. I know you have to go. I'll pay you the rest. Thank you so much. Take this,' she said, thrusting a small box into my hand. 'It's a present. I thought your wife might like it.'

Melvin walked towards me like he was about to punch me. 'Have you been fiddling with my wife's pipes?' he said, laughing. I ignored him, walked out and never went back.

As I was driving home, I opened the box Sophie had given me. Inside was a small magnifying mirror. It showed every flaw on your face. That was such a clever present. She was trying to drum up some business. Even I started considering doing something about the lines on my face when I looked at my magnified reflection. I realised then that Melvin was right. I had been a pawn in Sophie's grand plan. She knew exactly what she wanted, before I even walked in the door. She probably broke that toilet herself. I found out later she didn't even have a cleaning lady. She was a sixty-year-old secretary and her husband had just left her. She needed someone she could trust to help her turn her eighties porn palace in the poshest part of Paddington into a going concern. At the time I thought her businesses were a bit bizarre, but they were brilliant. She turned out to be the most entrepreneurial person I've ever worked for. She spotted a gap in an emerging market and she went for it. In case you are wondering, she also paid me the extra £5,000. She knew the modelling business and she ended up selling her agency to a big New York model-management company for millions. The consulting room I built for her was one of the first fully-functioning Botox studios in London. Botox had just become more accessible and the demand for it was massive. She is now one of the top consultants for anyone considering cosmetic surgery in London and, for a hefty fee, she still offers her clients a haven inside her house.

'That's quite a story,' said my friend, as we walked up Whitehall towards Trafalgar Square.

'As I said, lots of Londoners do something on the side to bring in a bit of extra cash. Accountants can also be acrobats. And secretaries can represent supermodels and help people to recover from serious cosmetic surgery.'

'And that all came from going to fix a broken toilet,' he said, as we crossed the road and ran for our respective night buses. 'See you next year,' I shouted, as the N91 bus pulled up and I joined the queue of pissed people trying to make their way safely home.

11

The Wine Story

As I've got older, I've become less motivated by money and more interested in learning. I get obsessed with things and try to find out as much as I can about that particular subject. For me, one of the best things about being self-employed is that I have been free to explore lots of other rare and wonderful worlds that I have come across. Over the years, I've done lots of things that have had nothing to do with plumbing. Some of the most fascinating have been for my mother-in-law, Miriam. I get on extremely well with her. In many ways, I get on with her better than Jo, but Miriam is a complicated character. She is fundamentally a very kind person; she just doesn't know how to show it. She loves her family very much and likes having them nearby, but she can also be very divisive and loves playing devil's advocate. Miriam is usually the root cause of most of her family's disagreements, without having a clue as to why. She drives them all crazy by tirelessly trading in guilt and is completely incapable of having a conversation without making some kind of cutting comment, which we all find very amusing. Most of Miriam's problems revolve around her complete inability to deal with money.

Fortunately, she has always been wealthy, although she doesn't like to admit it. On the one hand, she needs it, because it makes her feel secure; yet, on the other hand she loathes it, because she doesn't know what to do with it and it makes her feel set apart from everyone else, which makes her feel guilty.

Shortly after my father-in-law died, I was wedged under a kitchen sink in West Hampstead with a torch in my mouth, trying to replace a kitchen tap, when the guy I was working for told me he sold first-growth Burgundy and Bordeaux wines to a number of high-profile clients. As I was freeing his faucet, it occurred to me that he might be able to help sell my father-in-law's wine collection. So I asked him if he could point me in the right direction. When I eventually reappeared out of his kitchen cupboard, covered in washing powder because the carton had split as I reached for my wrench, he rather flippantly said, 'Send me a list of what you've got and I'll see what I can do.' I could see from the expression on his face that he thought my father-in-law probably had a couple of bottles of Blue Nun, which, as it happens, he did, but that wasn't the half of it. So, as I was driving away, I called Miriam to tell her the good news. Miriam was cooking gefilte fish in the kitchen of her house in Hampstead. Unfortunately, she was not a natural cook, but making gefilte fish was something she always did herself, and she would always get very flappy. 'Hi Nick,' she said, anxiously. I could hear her tipping the fish cakes into the frying pan as she spoke, the hot oil fizzed and spat. 'OH NO!' she screamed. 'Hang on, I need to get a cloth,' she said in a panic. 'Oh no, it's caught on fire – I'm having a complete nightmare.'

'Can I call you back?'

That's when I heard the smoke alarm go off and the phone went dead. Several hours later, she called back, sounding much calmer. 'Sorry about that. I've finished the gefilte fish – 75 balls of it – all ready for Passover. All by myself, no help as usual. I presume you are going to make an appearance at Passover this year?'

'We've never missed it once!' I said, rising to the bait.

I'm loving my new Quaker tap, by the way,' she said, changing the subject.

'It's a Quooker, not Quaker. They make porridge,' I replied, facetiously.

'Whatever. I've been showing it to everyone. They all think it's absolutely amazing. They can't believe what it can do,' she said, walking back over to demonstrate it to me, as if I could see what she was doing. 'Look, this way for normal hot and cold, this way for filtered, this way for sparkling and this for boiling. It's just amazing.'

'That's great,' I said, rolling my eyes.

'I do my bit, you know, drumming up work for my son-in-law.'

'Yes, thank you for that. The reason I was calling was because I've just been working for someone who works in the wine trade. He sells high-end claret. I was wondering if you'd like me to talk to him about the wine in the cellar down in Kent. He might be able to sell it for you.'

'Oh, don't be silly. Just leave it, let the builders have it!'

'Really?'

'Yes, it's all past its sell-by date,' she said.

'Are you sure?'

'Yes, I'm absolutely sure, but thank you for thinking of me. I'm sure it isn't worth anything. And even if it was, it would mean we'd have to bring it all back to London. Unless you haven't noticed, I'm in the process of trying to downsize, not that I'm getting much help!'

'We were there helping you all day on Sunday.'

'Whatever. The last thing I want is a load of dusty old wine bottles adding to the clutter. Ah, I'm going to have to go. I forgot Sacha was coming for tea and the house stinks of fish,' she said. At this time, Miriam was in the process of downsizing from her enormous house on the edge of Hampstead Heath to a significantly more modest large, five-bedroom house just around the corner from our tiny flat. This was supposedly so she could help us with our kids, even though our kids were way past the age of needing any help from their grandma. Jo and I were under no illusion that most of the help would be flowing in the other direction.

I let the wine idea go until I was reminded of it again a few months later when I walked into my plumbing merchant. John, the shop assistant, was sitting behind his desk staring at his computer. He was wearing a pair of ripped shorts, even though it was the middle of winter, a T-shirt which read, 'The customer is always … Yeah, right!' and a huge weightlifter's belt wrapped tightly round his waist.

'All right, John? What's with the belt?'

'Did my back in last night,' he said, winking.

'I'm after a new Torbeck valve.'

'Side or rear entry?'

'Rear entry.'

'That it?'

'No, a straight 4-inch male to female coupling, a bag of nipple nuts and a Surrey flange.'

'Push-fit coupling?'

'Yeah.'

'Need any lubricant?'

'No, I'll use washing up liquid.'

'Me too, since the missus went through the menopause! That it?'

'Yeah, I think so'.

'Paying or signing.'

'Signing.' As I walked out of the shop a huge lorry pulled up and blocked my van in. I sat there while the driver unloaded lots of boxes of wine and I remembered what the guy had said about sending him a list. I had the next day off, so I decided on a whim to drive down to Miriam's country house in Kent and pick up the wine from the cellar, so I could properly catalogue it. Once I'd driven down, I started to force-feed the jumble of unwanted wine into the back of my van, moving my tools and plumbing fittings to one side as I slowly filled it to the brim with old wooden wine boxes and single bottles wedged into every available space. It took me several hours. When I finished, there were over three hundred bottles wedged in with drills, angle grinders, jigsaws and nail guns, all carefully positioned to stop them from rolling around. As I drove back to London the mudguards scraped on the motorway, some of the bottles came unstuck and started to roll around, with siphons, plungers and old toilet seats falling all over them. When I eventually got back, I carefully carried them through our flat and put them in the shed at the end of the garden. I used the shed as my writing room so it was already full of lots of books and papers. By the time I had decanted all the wine out of the back of my van, I could hardly get into the shed. For the next week, I spent every spare moment I had listing the name and the year on each bottle of wine. Then I emailed the guy I had worked for in West Hampstead. His name was Aron.

Hi Aron,

Following on from our conversation, here is the list of wines that my mother-in-law is thinking of selling. I wonder if you could point us in the right direction?

All the best,
Nick the Plumber

Two minutes later, I received the following response: 'Are you serious!? She really has a case of 1945 Mouton Rothschild? What kind of plumber are you? This is not at all what I was expecting! Any chance I can come and have a look at it?'

I immediately called Miriam. 'I think I might have found someone to sell the wine,' I said, excitedly.

'I thought I told you to leave it for the builders.'

'You did, but I'm sorry, I just couldn't do that. I honestly think it might be worth some money. So, I went and picked it up.'

'When?'

'A couple of weeks ago.'

'Where is it now?'

'It's in the shed at the end of my garden. Did you know there were almost 300 bottles down there?'

'Really?'

'Yes. Anyway, you know I told you about that guy I was working for who deals in high-end claret? Well I just sent him the list and he wants to come and see it.'

'I feel there's a "but" coming.'

'I think he thinks that I might have stolen it.'

'You have, theoretically!'

'Hardly. What kind of thief rings you up to tell you that they've just catalogued your wine collection for you and then asks you if he can bring it over to your house, because he thinks he's found someone who might buy it?'

'Not a very good one, I'll give you that. No. I'm not having it here. I told you, I'm trying to get rid of stuff.'

'Look, I know you don't want it in your house, but presenting it in the shed at the end of my garden isn't exactly the best way of showing it. Especially since he already suspects that I've stolen it.'

'I don't care, it's not coming here.'

'If I put it neatly in your garage and explain it's just been moved here from the cellars of your country house, where it's been kept for the last twenty-five years, you never know, you might actually get some money for it.'

'I very much doubt it.'

'He's quite excited to see it.'

'Really?'

'He seems pretty keen.'

'Okay, but I want it out of here by the end of the month. I'm in the process of trying to simplify my life. Wherever I turn, there's just more and more stuff. It's a complete nightmare. No one's helping me. I'm thinking of getting someone in.'

'To do what?'

'To help me throw stuff away!'

'Miriam, we've been helping you loads with that! Look, I know this is hard, but think about it like this: you *are* simplifying your life, because you'll no longer have to worry about the wine.'

'I don't think I've ever worried about the wine – I don't drink!'

'Okay, but surely it would be better to sell it, rather than give it to the builders?'

'Okay. Okay, don't labour the point. Do I know this person? This person that you want to bring into my house?'

'No, not exactly, but I think you might have heard of him. He just got engaged to Linda Schulman's granddaughter,' I said, trying to put him into some kind of context that she might understand.

'Oh, I know Linda. Her mother was a good friend of my aunt. Has her granddaughter got engaged? I didn't know that. Is he nice?'

'Yes, he seems to be. It's a bit of a strange situation, really, since I was wedged under his kitchen sink for most of the time, but he seems to know his stuff.'

'What were you doing under his sink?'

'I was changing his kitchen tap.'

'Oh yes, of course. I forgot. What kind of tap?'

'Just a normal kitchen tap.'

'How much did it cost?'

'A hundred and twenty quid.'

'£120! And yet mine "apparently" cost £500!'

'It didn't "apparently" cost £500; it *actually* cost £500! Do you want me to show you the receipt? And you haven't actually paid me back for it yet.'

'Oh, haven't I? Well, I've been very busy. It's far too complicated. I keep putting sparkling water in my coffee. Anyway, this wine buyer of yours, when do you want to bring him over?'

'Whenever.'

'Well, I'm busy all of next week and most of the week after, but some time after that should be fine. Oh, hang on, no, I've got my Spanish lesson on Monday, I've got Pilates on Tuesday, Sacha is coming over for lunch on Wednesday, I'm going for a walk with Evelyn on Thursday and I think Virgin are coming on Friday to sort out the wi-fi, so maybe some time the week after that?'

'Okay, don't worry about it. I'll sort it out. I'll bring it over this weekend and put it neatly in your garage, then I'll arrange a time for him to come and see it. Don't worry, you don't have to be there. In fact, it might be better if you're not,' I said quietly under my breath, then I hung up and turned to Jo.

'Your mother is un-fucking-believable. I honestly don't know why I bother.'

'Is she being the sales prevention officer again?'

'All I'm trying to do is help her to sell the wine and yet she's constantly making me feel like I'm trying to steal from her.'

'You know Mum has a very screwed-up relationship with money.'

'That's because she's always had it,' I said, disappearing off to my man-shed.

Two weeks later, I arranged for Aron to come to Miriam's house to view the wine. I spent hours setting everything up. I even drove to Kent again and brought back several wine racks so I could display it properly. Unfortunately, despite all my best efforts, the garage was still in a complete state, full of old tape-machines and heaps of old wooden crates full of things from previous houses. Old family pictures that nobody wanted were piled up around the perimeter, and removal boxes that hadn't been opened for thirty years were stacked up in the middle of the room next to loads of cardboard boxes full of enough CDs, tapes and records to fill a small music shop. Miriam was supposed to be having her weekly hair appointment, but her hairdresser had cancelled at the last minute, which meant she was going to be in, which meant she would meet Aron before he saw the wine. Miriam was always the antagonist in her own story and she had a black belt in scuppering business deals. This made me extremely nervous. As Aron walked down the path towards her front door, I decided to deal with it head-on. 'Aron, this is my mother-in-law, Miriam. Don't worry, her bark is always much worse than her bite,' I said, opening the front door. Miriam completely ignored me and launched straight into her version of the Spanish inquisition. 'I understand you're marrying Linda Schulman's niece?'

'Yes, I am. Do you know her?'

'Linda was a very good friend of my aunt.'

'Oh, really? You must know Sylvie then?'

'Sylvie Schulman! Now there's a blast from the past. Yes, I think I went to school with her sister Leora.'

'Well, Sylvie is my girlfriend's mother.'

'I didn't really know Sylvie; she was a bit younger than Leora and me. Oh, how strange. What a small world!'

'Come and see the wine,' I said, trying to lure him away before Miriam said something stupid.

'I never really understood why my husband bought it. He didn't really drink. It used to make him sneeze.'

'So why *did* he buy it?' said Aron.

'He bought it as an investment,' I interrupted. 'He knew it would accumulate in value and when he came to sell it, it would be exempt from capital gains tax because the revenue view it as a depreciating asset,' I said, before Miriam had the chance to say anything.

'That's spot on. He was obviously a very clever man and now, I presume, you want to realise that investment?' he replied.

'Precisely.'

'Is that all true?' whispered Miriam, somewhat perplexed as we walked through to the garage.

'Yes,' I replied, as if to say, 'Now please shut the fuck up.'

'I had no idea. You see, I'm in the process of renovating our house in Kent and Nick didn't think it was a very good idea to leave it down there while the building work was going on. So, he brought it all up here. Without telling me, I hasten to add! Anyway, since it's here, I thought I might as well get it valued.'

'Well, I think he did you a bit of a favour,' said Aron, picking up a bottle and brushing his hand across its label.

'Are you interested in buying it yourself or for a client?' said Miriam, trying to appear a bit more switched on.

'Neither. I don't buy wine from private sources. I only buy directly from the châteaux.'

'Why's that?' she said, as if to say, 'Then why the hell are you here.'

'There are too many factors, particularly surrounding its storage, which makes buying it from private sources quite risky.'

'I'd be happy to show you the cellars at the house in Kent if you think that would be helpful,' I said, trying to take back control of the conversation. After that, Miriam lost interest and wandered back into the kitchen, leaving Aron and me to work our way through the bottles.

'Yes, possibly. Seeing the cellars might put peoples' minds at ease. I do have a few clients who do buy wine from private sources and I know they would love to have this,' he said, picking up a bottle and gently dusting it down to reveal the very old label with an ornate V in the design at the top.

'Which one is that?'

'This is a bottle of 1945 Mouton Rothschild. It is the only Mouton that was made entirely by women, because the men were all away fighting. It also happens to be one of the best vintages that Mouton Rothschild produced in the twentieth century. It's popular with the female gay community for obvious reasons. The V on the top of the bottle, with the wording *Année de la Victoire*, is to celebrate that it was bottled just after the end of the war.'

For the next five hours, he looked at every bottle and explained its history. It didn't take long for his enthusiasm to become infectious. I was soon completely engrossed. I had no idea that vintage wine could be so interesting or that there was so much to it. It depended on how hot the summer had been that year, how much rainfall there had been, when the grapes were picked, how long the wine had been kept before it was bottled, and how long it was kept in the bottle before it reached its maturity. The whole world of vintage wine absolutely fascinated me.

'Why don't you go through them and then pass them to me and I'll put everything that you think is good over here and everything that you think is bad over there,' I said, moving some of the boxes full of CDs and a trunkful of reel-to-reel master tapes, to try to make some more space.

'Wow! There aren't many of these left,' he said, handing me a bottle. 'One of these recently sold at Sotheby's in

New York for just over $5,000, and, as well as that, I see you also have an OWC. That's incredible.'

'What's an OWC?'

'It means it's in its original wine case. For a collector, it is like the holy grail. My God look at this, you've got a bottle of 1947 Cheval Blanc! This is also one of the best vintages of the twentieth century. You apparently used to be able to buy this for a reasonable amount of money in the late seventies and early eighties. As a result, most of it was drunk and now it's unbelievably rare. A bottle of this sold for nearly $15,000 at Christie's last month, and look! You've got five!'

'Is it okay?'

'Yes, it looks good. The colour is good. The cork is fine, the angel's share is correct,' he said, holding it up to the light. 'Yes, I think that can definitely go in the good pile. I feel like I've just broken into Tutankhamun's tomb. This is absolutely amazing. And your mother-in-law honestly had no idea?'

'Not a clue. She told me to leave it for the builders.'

Aron delved further into another wooden wine box. 'My God! This is a magnum of 1966 Pétrus. That's got to easily be worth £3,500. This is really popular with bankers at bonus time.'

'Because it's the year we won the World Cup?'

'Probably, but it was also a very good year.'

'Does that make it more valuable?'

'What? The year? Or the World Cup?'

'The World Cup.'

'Yes, it can do. Basically, it's all about supply and demand. There's not much 1966 Pétrus around now, but the demand is still high.'

'What about this one?' I said, pointing to a wooden box that was falling apart and held together with several pieces of string.

'Oh, my God! This is very special indeed. This is an OWC of 1939 Château Lafite.' He sat down, clutching one of the bottles to his chest as he recounted the story. 'When the Nazis invaded France, the owners of Château Lafite ordered part of the cellars to be bricked up to stop the Nazis from stealing their best wine. But this wasn't enough, so they apparently sunk some cases into the lake in front of the château as well. I think this could be one of those cases and if it is, it's extremely rare. Put this over there, I'll carefully look through it later. As you can see, a lot of the labels are damaged.'

'Does that affect their value?' I asked, sheepishly.

'Yes, but in this case, given the story behind it, it would be a miracle if they weren't, so it shouldn't affect its value too much.'

'How about those two bottles over there?'

'These are two magnums of 1960 Krug champagne, very nice, nothing wrong with them. My God, this is an unopened OWC of 1960 Dom Pérignon, which is obviously very popular with James Bond fans. This is a case of 1970 Haut-Brion, which is missing one bottle but it all looks good. This is a magnum of 1972 Cristal champagne and it's *good*. Wow, here's a bottle of 1929 Mouton Rothschild! I've never seen one that old! Oh, what a shame! It's gone. You see, the cork's perished and half the wine has seeped out. The angel's share is far too big,' he said, holding it up to the light. 'What a shame. Mind you, it's almost a hundred years old.'

'How long can it last?'

'Top class claret like this can easily last fifty or sixty years. Some can last longer, but it really starts to depreciate quite rapidly from then on. This is a magnum of 1947 Margaux and another of 1967 Lafite. My God, this is absolutely unbelievable! I have honestly never seen a collection of wine this good. It's utterly breathtaking!'

'How much do you think it might all be worth?'

'I'll have to go through it, but from what I've seen so far, this could easily be worth a hundred and fifty thousand pounds, maybe more!'

'Really? Fucking hell!'

'What's that?' he said, pointing to a case by my feet. I passed it over to him and he dusted it off.

'What is it?' I said, excitedly.

'It's a case of 1969 Frascati.'

'What's that worth?' I said, hardly able to contain my excitement.

'Absolutely nothing. This shouldn't have been drunk then, let alone now! But I do have a client who I think may be interested in buying some of the good stuff. He used to be the wine buyer for Harrods, but now he's the private wine buyer for a Russian oligarch.'

'That's great, but I think I'm going to get Sotheby's and Christie's to value it first.' I said.

'You're probably right. I'm sure they will bite your arm off to get their hands on a collection like this. You know, this might be the best collection to come onto the market since Andrew Lloyd Webber sold his a few years ago.'

'Okay, give me a few weeks to get the valuations, then let's see what your guy is prepared to offer us for it. I think we'd rather sell the whole lot in one go rather than split it up and sell it one bottle at a time. Do you think he might be interested in buying the lot?'

'Possibly. He certainly won't mess around. He knows what every vintage is worth. He buys over a million pounds worth of wine every year. I'll send him the list and let's see what he says.'

'Okay, sounds like a plan. If he does decide to buy it, how much do you want for the introduction?'

'I'll leave that up to you,' he said, knowing full well that he was putting me in a very difficult position. I knew that trick; I sometimes used it myself.

I spent the next two weeks negotiating firstly with Sotheby's, then Christie's and then with Aron's client. After a number of very difficult discussions, we finally agreed on a price and sold it all to Aron's client. It was all contingent on him viewing the wine and it all being in good order, so I arranged a time for him to come and view it, and made sure it was when Miriam was out playing bridge.

When he arrived, he didn't look anything like what I thought he would. Instead of being a large, heavy-set man with a thick neck and powerful hands, he was actually quite slight, with delicate features and astute eyes. 'Hello, my name is David,' he said, as I opened Miriam's front door. 'We've been emailing each other. It's nice to finally put a face to the name. So, you're the man who's been driving such a hard bargain. I hope you don't mind, but I've come dressed for packing,' he said, pointing to his designer jeans.

'Not at all. I'm very pleased to meet you,' I said, holding out my hand. 'Shall we go through.' Over the course of the next six-and-half hours, David carefully checked every bottle. He bounced some, but took quite a few of the bottles that were in the 'may need to be tested' pile. Eventually, after a final 'to and fro' over the price, we agreed on a final figure and he gave me a cheque, made out to Miriam. Then he carefully started to box it all up and packed it into the back of his temperature-controlled van. There were no old toilet seats or impact drivers in the back of *his* van! I smiled at the image of how I had transported the wine back to London a month earlier. Once that was all over, Aron, who had been there all day, was about to leave, when Miriam arrived back from playing bridge. I quickly grabbed her and took her to one side before she had a chance to introduce herself to David. 'I think we should give Aron something for introducing us.'

'I thought his client was paying him?'

'Regardless, I think we should offer to give him some money to say thank you.'

'Really? How much?'

'Well, if we'd sold it at auction, we would have had to pay ten per cent commission to the auction house.'

'As much as that?'

'They wanted 17.5 per cent, but I eventually managed to get them down to 10 per cent. On top of that, the buyer would also have had to pay another 10 per cent buyer's premium. That's how I got him to pay a bit more than he initially wanted to.'

'Really, I didn't know you'd done that.'

'Yes, his first offer was almost thirty thousand less than we eventually got.'

'Really! How much did we get?'

'A hundred and eighty-five thousand.'

'Pounds?'

'Yes. Look. Here's the cheque.'

'My God, what on earth am I going to do with that?' she exclaimed, clearly in a state of shock.

'Still think you should have left it for the builders? Look, I don't think you should give him as much as 10 per cent. After all, I did most of the legwork, but I do think you should give him something.'

'Whatever you think,' she said.

Aron was in his car ready to leave. I ran out just as he was about to drive off. He wound down his window and I said, 'How's the tap, by the way?'

'It's great. Who'd have thought that this would all come from a plumbing problem!'

'I know,' I said, laughing, 'Mad, isn't it? If you send me your bank details, I'll get Miriam to transfer you some money to say thank you for introducing us to David. We really appreciate it.'

'Thank you – it's been an absolute pleasure and a great story to tell. One day you should write it down.'

'I will,' I said, as he drove off.

When I got back into the house, Miriam was just coming downstairs. 'Now, introduce me to this mysterious wine buyer of yours!' she said, walking over to introduce herself.

'Hello, I'm Miriam. I hear you've decided to buy my husband's wine collection,' she said, striding into the garage. 'What on earth are you going to do with it all?'

'Pleased to meet you, my name is David Katz.'

'You're not one of the Manchester Katzes, are you? It's just that my aunt was a Manchester Katz. Her father owned the Katz department store.'

'Oh, really? My grandfather worked for them.'

'My aunt grew up in a large house, not far from Chatsworth.'

'I've been to that house. My grandfather showed it to me.'

'Oh, how strange. So how are you related to Aunty Adele? Come into the house. I have a copy of the family tree.' David stopped what he was doing and followed Miriam back into the house. My heart sank. Miriam never missed an opportunity to find a new relative; it was her favourite pastime. I could see that this might go on for hours. It wouldn't be long before she was telling him all about how they had left Russia during the pogroms; how her great-grandmother had married her husband's great-grandfather; how they had had twelve children, and she had died of exhaustion. I'd heard it all before, but stopping Miriam in full flow, was like trying to stop a runaway freight train, so I rolled my eyes and let her get on with it, fearing that at any minute she would hit the buffers and all my hard work would be for nothing.

'Right,' said Miriam, taking down an enormous scroll from the top of the bookcase. 'Okay, this is me. And this is Aunty Adele. Now, where are you?'

'Okay,' he said, carefully studying the scroll. 'So, your aunt's father Samuel was my great-grandfather's brother. You see, it's not filled in properly, but this is my great-grandfather Isaac, who had two children, one of whom was my grandfather, who in turn had three children, one of whom is my father, who in turn had me and my brother.'

'Oh, how fascinating. That's wonderful,' I interjected, trying to bring the genealogical gathering to a close – all to no avail.

'Oh, I'm so pleased it's staying in the family,' continued Miriam, ignoring all my best efforts. 'So, what is it you intend to do with all this wine? You're not an alcoholic, are you?'

'Not at all, I don't drink.'

'Then why are you buying it?'

'Well, some of it will go into my boss's private collection and the rest will go into a new shop that we are opening near Berkeley Square.'

'Oh, really? I love Berkeley Square. I don't recall there being a wine shop, though.'

'We haven't opened yet.'

'I shall have to visit it next time I'm in town.'

'You must stop by. In fact, I will send you an invitation to our grand opening in a couple of weeks. Now, if you will excuse me, I still have quite a lot of wine to pack and it's getting late.'

Several hours later, I arrived home, utterly exhausted, and collapsed into my favourite armchair. Jo had just finished cooking dinner for the kids and was dishing up.

'Fish fingers, chips and peas! My favourite!' I said, pouring myself a large glass of wine and stealing a chip off my son's plate.

'So how did it go?' she said, pouring herself a glass of Vouvray and sitting down opposite me.

'He got there at 8.30 this morning and he didn't leave until about an hour ago. He checked every single bottle, bounced a few, but took some others, so, over all, it went well. Your mother was a nightmare, but we got through it. She didn't manage to sabotage it. After a lot of toing and froing he eventually agreed to take the lot, give or take a few bottles.'

'Great. How much did you get?'

'Just over a hundred and eighty-five grand.'

'Fuck!'

'I know.'

'Thank you so much for doing that for her. She's bloody lucky to have you as a son-in-law,' she said, leaning in to kiss me.

'If only she could show it!' I said, 'but it's nice to hear someone say it!'

Two weeks later, I walked into my plumbing merchant.

'All right, John? Are you open over Christmas?'

'Yeah, not the bank holidays, but the rest of the time we'll be open. Oh, that reminds me, I've got something for you,' he said, grabbing one of the boxes of wine from behind his desk. 'What do you want? Red, or white?'

'Red.'

'Good choice. The white's a pile of pants. We really pushed the boat out this year, not the usual crap, we've spent a fiver a bottle! Happy Christmas!'

'Cheers, John,' I said, taking the box and putting it into the back of my van where £185,000 of vintage wine had sat a month before!

12

The War Rooms

For me, the best bit about being a plumber is getting to know the people I work for. I'm lucky because most of my clients keep calling me, so I get to see their lives play out, too, albeit from underneath their kitchen sink. I love hearing what's happened to them since I last saw them. Over the years, I've watched hundreds of people climb the property ladder and every time they moved to a new house, I usually ended up building them a new bathroom. I often recount their stories to family and friends, but it never occurred to me that telling one of their stories would help me to unblock a problem I was having at home, yet it did. And it happened in the most bizarre way.

Several years ago, I took the day off to spend some time with my teenage daughter. Things had been very strained between us for quite some time. I offered to take her to the Churchill War Rooms as she was studying the Second World War for GCSE. We sat in silence as the bus slowly wound its way through the busy London streets. She was plugged into her headphones and I spent most of the journey trying to think of something to say. It was raining outside and the windows were covered with condensation. Bad weather always looks worse through a window, I thought, as we pulled up outside Charing Cross. Now I wasn't so sure. The rain was pelting down and the puddles on the pavement were converging and cascading over the kerb. Maybe walking would help to break the ice, I thought, as we got off the bus. Part of me was dreading it. I knew she was, too. I could see it on her face. She wasn't really interested in the Churchill War Rooms; she was just humouring me. She kept lagging behind, looking at her phone under her raincoat. It was ironic that I had chosen the War Rooms because our own war was still raging. Or at least it was in my head. We were two storytellers trapped in a tiny flat in constant combat over who got to tell the tale.

She saw things her way, and I saw them mine. We were both too needy. Too sensitive. Too dramatic. Too explosive. Whenever we spoke, I felt like a rhino running down a hill with a very delicate vase balancing on my back. The more we talked, the faster I ran, but at the bottom of the hill there was an impenetrable wall. I crashed into it every time. The vase shattered and Jo spent the next two days trying to put it back together. The truth is, I didn't know how to handle her. I felt like I only opened my mouth to change feet. I wasn't prepared for an intelligent, young, woke woman who had all the same faults as me, but with oodles of oestrogen thrown in. I had absolutely no insight into a teenage girl's brain. She was holding a mirror up to me, and she didn't even know it. So, when she needed me the most, I withdrew and let Jo handle it.

She's probably going to storm off and tell Jo she hates me, that's the usual routine, I thought, as we walked down Whitehall. Still neither of us said a word. So, in a moment of madness, I started to tell her one of my plumbing stories. That was always my default position, but to my surprise, this time, she actually listened. And, as I painted the picture, more and more of the details came flooding back to me and I began to realise just how relevant it all was.

'The art is to die well,' I said, crossing the road in front of The Cenotaph.

'What do you mean by that?' she said, briefly looking up from her phone. She really was very beautiful, but maybe all fathers think the same of their daughters.

'The best way is to die broke,' I said, relieved I'd finally broken the ice and got her attention.

'What, like a tramp in the street?'

'No, not exactly.'

'Why? What's wrong with having lots of money?'

'Because, when you die, everything you own is added up and anything over a certain amount is taxed.' Talking to her about the intricacies of inheritance tax probably isn't the most sensible subject, I thought, as we stopped to peer down Downing Street.

'But haven't you already paid tax on it?'

'Yes, that's just how it works.'

Quick, change the subject. You're losing her. Think of something else.

'So, when you die, am I going to have to pay tax on our flat?'

'No, hopefully not.'

She's still with me. Think of something that will hook her in, for God's sake, think!

'Why?'

'Because Mum and I are going to try to give it to you seven years before we die, or at least that's the plan.'

'But how will you know? No one knows when they're going to die.'

This is amazing. She's actually engaged. We're having a conversation. Okay, it's about inheritance tax. It's not ideal, but it's a start!

'That's true. As soon as Mum and I turn seventy, and hopefully we won't die before then, we're going to transfer it over to you and your brother.'

'Wow, thanks, Dad. How old are you now?'

'Fifty.'

'So, in twenty years, you're going to give me the flat?'

'Yes. There is one proviso though.'

I've got it. Money. Talk to her about money. She loves money.

'What?'

'You have to promise you will look after us.'

'Of course,' she said, looking at the floor.

I didn't believe her, but I carried on anyway. 'Well, you'd be surprised. I was working for someone a few years ago, who didn't do that, and he ended up giving almost a million pounds to the government.'

'Why would he do that?'

'Are you sure you want to know?'

This is unheard of. We haven't spoken for this long in years. I was starting to get really nervous, trying to remember the story, moulding it in my mind.

'Go on,' she sighed. 'I know you're going to tell me anyway. I've finished on Snapchat now.'

I'm losing her. Keep it pithy. Don't get bogged down in the detail.

My brain was accelerating. The rhino was about to run. I knew once I started, I wouldn't be able to stop. It was going to be a disaster. Jo wasn't there to put her back together. *Where's the wall? Slow down. Don't charge ahead.*

Go at her speed. Let her be in charge. 'He held onto all his money and didn't give any of it away until it was too late.'

'But surely having money is a good thing,' she said, as we walked towards the Treasury.

She's going with it. Maybe she wants this to work as much as I do?

'Not always. Being rich when you're old can be problematic.'

'Maybe he was selfish and always put his needs first?'

'Yes, he did. That's very perceptive of you.'

She's clever. She's always been clever. Maybe she's too clever? I thought, as we walked down the steps towards the War Rooms.

'But he also didn't want to be a burden. He had always been in charge and that's a very difficult thing to give up,' I said, as I opened the door at the bottom of the stairs. As she walked in, it occurred to me that I was fighting for my family, just like all the people who worked there during the war. I was just doing it in a much less warlike way.

'The way I see it, life is like a relay race,' I said, as we joined the queue.

Treat her like a lady. Behave like a gentleman. If she says something arsey, just ignore it, she doesn't realise she's doing it. She's just anxious. Above all STAY CALM.

'The way I see it, you have to try to accumulate as much as you can, then hand it over to your kids seven years before you drop down dead.'

'Why seven years?'

'If you give it away seven years before you die, then your children don't have to pay tax on it. It's just the rules. I don't know why. Anyway, I want to see what you'll do with it,' I said, showing the receptionist our tickets. We wandered through the narrow passageway that led to the first room, listening to the tour guide on our separate headsets. I couldn't take my eyes off her. Her brain was like an enormous sponge. I could see it absorbing all the information, analysing and storing it. She has a phenomenal memory. At the end of the first room she could tell me word for word exactly what the tour guide had said. Then, she asked me the most insightful questions. I didn't know any of the answers, so it occurred to me that we should play a game.

'I won't listen to my headset. You tell me what the tour guide says, and I'll tell you what happened to my client,' I said, as we walked into the second room.

'Okay, you go first,' she said.

This is brilliant. Better than I ever imagined, I thought, as she sat down next to me. She looked like my mum. She had the same inquisitive look. The same light bluey-green eyes. The same sadness in them. I wanted to hug her, but it was too soon for that, so I continued to tell her about my client. It was safer that way.

'Layla was one of my best customers. She was obsessed with property porn.'

'Dad!'

'It's just an expression,' I said, laughing. 'It means she watched all the property programmes on TV. She didn't masturbate over them, or at least I don't think she did!' She rolled her eyes. I loved it when she did that. 'Although, come to think of it, she did have a bit of thing for Phil Spencer!' For a split second, I thought she was going to put her head on my shoulder, like she used to when she was a little girl, but she pulled back at the last minute, so I carried on. 'Layla was never satisfied. She always wanted more. As soon as she finished renovating her house, she sold it and bought a bigger one. She was brilliant at it. She had great taste, she always got a good deal and she knew how to add value. She wanted to be a property developer, but she didn't have enough money, so she was confined to renovating her own home. I used to joke that every time I went to the toilet, the room had changed colour! She was very quick-witted, and she was always looking for a double entendre. Plumbing provided her with a lot of inspiration. Anything with the word 'pipe' in it for a start!' My daughter rolled her eyes again, but didn't say anything.

Maybe I'm part of the problem, I thought. I always take over. I never let her speak.

'She found it funny that north London was full of lots of frustrated housewives.'

'Why?' she said, smiling at me.

'Because it *isn't*! It's a *Carry On* cliché. Anyway, when it came to work, she knew what she wanted. She was very pragmatic, and she never messed about with money. Her father had a small property portfolio, which she looked after, so she kept me pretty busy. Layla was super-connected. She was in with all the mums in Muswell Hill. Whenever one of her friends had a plumbing problem, she gave them my number. If I'd paid her a commission for every job I got from her, it would have come to a lot of money, but she never asked me for a penny. So, when she asked me to replace a bathroom in a flat near Sloane Square, I made sure I was available.'

'How did she buy a flat if she didn't have any money?'

'Good question. Her father gave her the money. But we're getting ahead of ourselves. Right, now it's your turn,' I said, slamming on the brakes before I got too carried away.

We walked into the next room. My daughter pressed play on her headset, and I wandered through the room looking at all the photographs, reading the occasional footnote. Then I sat down and waited for her to finish. She took ages. She read everything and listened to all the commentary. I was beginning to think she was just trying to avoid me, that she found me boring and didn't want to hear my silly plumbing story, but then she walked up to me, smiled and said, 'It's fascinating. You know the secretaries knew Churchill was here because they could smell his cigar. I can't believe he smoked cigars down here! It must have been unbearable. You know one cigar is equivalent to twenty cigarettes. It was okay for him to smoke his cigars, but their typewriters all had to be silenced. Typical. Men, they're so selfish!'

She was right. Most men *are* selfish. I knew I was. I expected her to fit into my life, yet I didn't want to fit into hers. 'You know they only moved down here because Downing Street was bombed. But they kept it quiet. They didn't want anyone to know.' I knew what it was like to have a bomb go off at home and not tell anyone. How strange that we were visiting the place that Churchill went after it happened to him. 'Come on, it's your turn. What happened next,' she said, encouraging me to continue.

'Are you sure you want to know?'

'Yes, you can't leave me dangling.'

'It was a top-floor flat in an old mansion block at the end of Sloane Street. There was an ageing gentility to the place. Noel Coward lived there in the 1930s. It had one of those old caged lifts, like the one in *Thoroughly Modern Millie*. It smelled of the kind of old-fashioned perfume that some widows wear. There was an understated grandeur to the flat. It was the kind of place a Lord would live when he was in London. The porter was a short, red-faced Irishman called Connor. He had high blood pressure and

222

a complexion like the inside of a coffee pot. No one did anything unless Connor said so. His desk was opposite the front door. All the old ladies loved him. He was flamboyant in a conservative kind of a way. He wore brightly coloured cravats and patent-leather shoes, but, to me, he was a complete bastard. Shall we go into the next room?'

'No, carry on, I'm enjoying it.'

'There was a small parking area at the back of the building, but, when I got there, it had a chain across it with a padlock. Connor had the key, so I drove round to the front of the building and rang the bell. He was sitting behind his desk reading his newspaper. It's funny because he looked a lot like Churchill. He was a short, squat man with a fat face that hid his frown. He had the same determined mouth that never smiled and teeth that were stained from drinking too much red wine. He fiddled with his cufflinks, then pressed the buzzer on the side of his desk.'

'Hi …,' I said, smiling.

'You can't park there!' he said, interrupting me.

'I've been asked …,' I continued, trying to be as polite as possible.

'That's as may be. But you can't park there,' he retorted.

There was a short silence while I considered what to do next.

'Move it!' he screamed, suddenly standing up. His face looked like it was about to burst.

'I've been asked by Layla Freeman; she owns the penthouse,' I stammered.

'I don't care! You can't park there!' he shouted, moving towards me. I turned around and immediately ran back to my van and moved it, parking it on a double yellow line further down the road.

'What do you want?' he said, buzzing me back in a few minutes later.

'I've come to look at the bathroom.'

'Who sent you?'

'Layla.'

'Is she the lass who likes renting to foreigners?' he said, interrupting me again.

'Possibly,' I said, nervously.

I could tell that he didn't like her. But, as I was soon to find out, Connor didn't like anyone. He was a bigoted imperialist, who disliked anyone who didn't have a double-barrelled surname.

'I don't like anyone dodgy working in my building!' he shouted.

'I'm not dodgy. I live in Crouch End!' I replied, as if it was ludicrous to suggest that anyone who lived in Crouch End would ever do anything dodgy.

'I don't care where you come from,' he screamed, as if he'd just swallowed something particularly unpleasant. I didn't know what to say to that, so I ignored it and stuck to the point. 'I was wondering if you had the key to the parking area around the back?'

'There aren't any spaces,' he said, abruptly.

'But I just drove past it. It's empty.'

'If I say there aren't any spaces, there aren't any bloody spaces!' he shouted, standing up and stepping out from behind his desk.

When I got back to my van, a parking warden, with a patch over one eye, was writing me out a ticket.

'Oh, come on, mate,' I appealed to him.

'Sorry,' he said, wedging the ticket under my windscreen wiper.

It was my second parking ticket in less than a week, so I called Layla and told her what had happened.

'Okay, leave it with me,' she said.

A few minutes later, she called me back.

'Someone apparently has to vouch for you,' she said.

'Well, can you call him? I've just got a parking ticket! It's already cost me £70 and I haven't even seen the place.'

'He doesn't like me. We had an argument about renting the flat. Everyone's undesirable according to him. He's a racist pig, who drinks too much and only talks to toffs.'

'That's good to know,' I said, sarcastically. 'But can you please call him and ask him if I can park at the back of the building. There really isn't anywhere to park around here.'

'It won't help. Don't worry, one of my dad's friends lives there. She gets on really well with him. I'll get her to vouch for you,' she said, putting down the phone.

Two minutes later, she called me back. 'She's not there at the moment. She's out shopping, so leave it for today and I'll sort it out tomorrow. Oh, by the way, I'm told he's partial to a decent single malt. Not your normal supermarket shit. He's a real connoisseur, he likes the really rare stuff.'

At this point in my narrative, my daughter stood up and I followed her into the next room. 'Nazi propaganda! I wasn't expecting that,' I said, changing the subject to encourage her to take her turn. 'Churchill depicted as an alcoholic imperialist. The Treaty of Versailles caused the war. That wasn't what I was taught at school. Nothing about the Hun and their evil empire-building?' I whispered, as I walked past her.

'We have a much more balanced view nowadays,' she replied.

'Probably because your grandparents didn't fight in it,' I replied, trying to find somewhere to sit.

'That's true. The more time passes the easier it is to see what really happened,' she said, moving on to the next exhibit.

Maybe she's right. Maybe we just need some time, then we'll see what really happened to us, I thought, as I watched her walk around the room.

'Stalin did a deal with Hitler,' she said, sitting down next to me. 'If Hitler hadn't broken that pact, he would probably have won the war.'

'I didn't know that. I should have paid more attention at school,' I said, astonished at my own ignorance. 'Did you know all this before?'

'Yes, we're learning about it in history. What happened when you went back to the flat?' she said, encouraging me to continue with my plumbing story.

'The next day I turned up with a bottle of the rarest whiskey I could find. Connor was sitting behind his desk wearing a sports jacket and a red paisley cravat. He looked like Toad of Toad Hall on holiday in the tropics. I sheepishly rang the bell and he walked towards me like he was going to punch me. 'What's that?' he said, pointing at the bottle.

'I'm told you're partial to a wee dram,' I said, smiling.

'Get out!' he said, slamming the door in my face.

I went back to my van and called Layla.

'Not again,' she said. 'Look. Talk to Mrs Nicholson. I'll text you her number.'

As soon as the text came through, I called the number. Mrs Nicholson answered it immediately. She was a New Yorker with a clipped way of speaking. She clearly didn't suffer fools gladly. 'Meet me in the foyer,' she said, hanging up. When I got to the front door, she opened it. 'You must be the plumber,' she said, looking me up and down. 'Connor likes to be appreciated after you've done the job. Not before! Don't worry. I've apologised for your appalling lack of etiquette. He told me to give you this,' she said, handing me the key to the padlock. 'And for God's sake don't antagonise him any more, otherwise your life won't be worth living.'

Ten minutes later, I walked back round to the front of the building and pressed the bell. Connor stood up and walked slowly towards me, saying, 'Don't ever try to bribe me again. If it wasn't for Mrs Nicholson, you'd be on your bike,' he said, opening the door. 'Give it to me when you've finished,' he whispered under his breath.

'Shall I carry on?' I said to my daughter.

'Yes, I'm enjoying it,' she said, sweetly.

So I continued:

'The flat was like a downsized version of Downton Abbey. There were ostrich feathers in the hall. It had large mahogany doors and a big bay window. In the sitting room there was an enormous carved limewood fireplace, which looked as if it had been taken from a stately home and, around it, were three high-sided antique sofas covered in tapestry with tasselled ropes holding them together. The flat had only one bedroom. Liberace would have loved it. It had a four-poster bed with gold pineapples carved into all four corners. Bright yellow curtains hung at the window and the walls were covered in gilt wallpaper. The whole place was crammed full of antiques. The man who had lived there had been a friend of Mrs Nicholson. That's how Layla had found out about it. He had been an Italian Viscount, who had died suddenly, leaving no next of kin, so it was a probate purchase.'

'What's that?' my daughter asked.

'It means she bought it off the government. If you die without a will, and you don't have any children, everything goes to the government, which is ironic, but we'll get to that. There was absolutely nothing wrong with it. It had a kind of shabby chic charm to it. Layla was renting it to a small Japanese man with a monobrow while she figured out what she was going to do to it. He was a strange fish. The nervous type. Anxious. Never looked you in the eye. He lived alone with a sphynx cat called Kai.'

'What's a sphynx cat?'

'It's a cat that doesn't have any fur. As soon as he opened the door, I knew he was going to be difficult.'

'"Can you take your shoes off," he said, fidgeting uncomfortably. "I have a dust allergy," he went on, showing me through the grand reception room. I got the feeling he really didn't want me to be there.'

'"Have you just moved in?" I said, trying to make conversation.'

'"No, I've been here for a few months," he replied, opening the bathroom door.'

'I was totally gobsmacked. It was without doubt the best bathroom I'd ever seen. There was a huge chandelier hanging in the centre of the room with a pristine roll-top bath sitting underneath it. There was a mahogany vanity unit with a large sink with big brass taps and beautiful hand-painted tiles on the wall behind it. Above it, there was a huge gold mirror with two 1920s' Lalique wall lights with clouded glass shades. Opposite the door was an exquisite high-level WC with a thick black wooden seat and an ornately decorated copper cistern with a coat of arms engraved into it.'

'Calm down, Dad! You're describing it like it turned you on,' said my daughter, smiling.

'It did! A good bathroom always does it for me! It was utterly breathtaking. I couldn't believe Layla wanted me to change it. As I stood there, it dawned on me that I could be standing in Noel Coward's bathroom. I could see him standing right in front of me. Dressed in tails, his hair carefully combed. He was about to leave. His play was about to premiere in Piccadilly. All the press were going to be there. He'd show them. He'd show them all. He'd be the toast of the town. He looked at himself in the mirror, slipped on his shoes, picked up a cane from the hat stand in the hall and left.'

'"Can you make sure you keep the door closed if you're going to be making a mess?" said the tenant, bringing me back to reality. Then he opened a cupboard, took out a vacuum cleaner and started to hoover where I had just walked.'

'Why did he do that?'

'I have no idea. He was clearly a cleanliness freak. I took out my phone and called Jo. I could hardly contain my excitement. She had been on at me for years to replace our bathroom.'

'I remember. Can we have a break now?' my daughter said, standing up and walking towards the next room. I found it hard, stopping like that, but she was probably right, otherwise I would have carried on for ages. It was her turn. She pressed play on her headset and I followed her into the next room, listening over her shoulder. How else will I know she's telling me the truth, I thought, as I shadowed her around the room. *Maybe you should trust her, stop trying to micromanage her, leave her alone, she's a young adult, stop treating her like she's a child,* I thought, as I wandered off and waited for her to finish.

'Churchill's wife came to stay regularly. They had an apartment upstairs, but when there was an air raid, she'd come down. Did you see the stairs? She even had her own bedroom and her own dining room down here. It must have been like living in a crypt. If it had been bombed, no one would have got out of here alive,' she said, walking towards the café.

'What do you fancy? How about a cup of hot chocolate?' I said, following her.

'Oh, thanks, Dad. Yes, please. Then you can tell me what happened next.'

She won't be able to keep it up. I'm bound to mess it up soon, there's no way we're going to make it all the way round without her exploding about something, I thought, as I paid the man for the hot chocolate and walked over to the table she had chosen.

'You know what they say. Shoemaker's children never have decent shoes!' I said, sitting down opposite her. She was so relaxed. The beautiful, brilliant young girl, who played Peter Pan in her primary-school play, was back. All her teenage angst had disappeared. 'I knew exactly what Mum wanted,' I said, trying to remember where I was in the story as I watched her sip her hot chocolate. 'One of the benefits of being a plumber is you never have to buy your own bathroom. You simply recycle one that would otherwise have ended up in a skip.'

'Is that why our flat is full of old crap?'

'It's not crap, it's Bohemian!'

'Whatever,' she said, smiling.

'So, I delayed all my other work and I told Layla I could start it straight away. As I was taking my tools up to the flat, I kept bumping into Connor in the corridor. It was weird. I'd never worked anywhere with a porter before.

'The next day, Ryan didn't turn up, so I was late. Connor was sitting at his desk with a face like a spanked arse.'

My daughter just looked at me, but she didn't say anything. She didn't need to. The look was enough. I could see what she was thinking: *Stop it, Dad. Stop always trying to shock me.*

'It's just an expression. He had high blood pressure. His face was always flushed,' I said, trying to justify myself. 'When I got back to my van, the same parking warden was writing me out another ticket.'

'"Oh, come on, mate! I was just getting the key to the parking area," I explained to him.'

'"You can't park here. You should know that by now!" he said, handing me the ticket.'

'My plan was to un-plumb everything then schlep it across London to our flat. But, without Ryan, there was no way I could carry it downstairs. Let's have a break. It's your turn to educate me,' I said, standing up.

We walked into the next room and she turned on her headset. I found a sofa near the exit. She read everything and then sat down next to me.

'My legs hurt,' she said, slipping off her shoes.

'No wonder,' I said, pointing to her platform heels. 'What did you find out?'

'We wouldn't have won if it wasn't for the Russians. Did you know twenty-four million Russians died during the war. The Germans only lost six-and-half million. The Japanese 2.6 million. We lost fewer than half a million. The Americans, 400,000. A total of eighty-five million people died. It's like the whole world went mad. Did you know twenty million Chinese people died? They were our ally.'

'I didn't know that. Shall I carry on or do you want a break?'

'No, don't stop, I want to know what happened.'

'As I dismantled the bathroom, I soon realised most of it was useless. The toilet didn't flush properly. The vanity unit was rotten. I could see why Layla wanted me to replace it. It looked great, but it was all falling apart. In the end the only thing I managed to salvage was the bath. The next day, Ryan turned up with the word "Ale" cut into one side of his hair.'

'"What's going on?" I said, somewhat taken aback.'

'"Me mate cut me 'air last night," he said, nonchalantly.'

'"What's with the word?"'

'"He's working in a barber down Brixton. They all want Zs cut into their afros, so he practised on me."'

'"Why Ale?"'

'"Because I like it," he said, rolling himself a fag. I didn't care, but, when we arrived at the flat, Connor wouldn't let him in because he looked like a lout, so I had to send him home. Talk about work prevention officer! I opened the window in the bathroom and started to take all the tiles off the walls. The plaster crumbled and the room soon filled with dust. I couldn't see what I was doing, so I opened the bathroom door. I was hoping it would help to blow the dust out of the window. By lunchtime every corner of the flat was covered in dust. The tenant was totally traumatised. He started manically jumping up and down, screaming at me in Japanese. So, I had to spend the rest of the day cleaning the flat, trying to calm him down. But, although I didn't know it, things were about to get a lot worse!'

'The next day Ryan turned up with the word, "Tabs" shaved into the other side of his head.'

'This time he had brought a hat, but it didn't make any difference. Connor still wouldn't let him in. So, I was once again forced to work alone. I stuck polythene over all the doors, covered all the carpets and put brand-new dust sheets over all the furniture, but it didn't make any difference. The tenant still complained.'

'"He's demanding that we put him up in a hotel," said Layla, when she called me that evening.'

'"I swear there's nothing more I can do."'

'"Don't worry, I've booked him into a B&B, but they won't let him take his cat. He's going to have to leave it in the flat. Can you feed it and change its litter tray?"'

'"Can't he come back to do that?"'

'"I thought you'd jump at the chance, otherwise you'll have to clean the flat before you leave," said Layla.'

'"I just can't take responsibility for the cat – he'll have to come and check on it," I replied.'

'The next day, when I arrived, all the residents were standing outside. "What's going on?" I said, jumping out of my van.'

'"The fire alarm went off," said Connor.'

'"Is everything all right?"'

'"No. There's been a fire in the penthouse," he said, looking at me accusingly. My heart skipped a beat. The cost of repairing a building like this would be eye-watering and my public liability insurance probably wouldn't cover it. I started manically pacing up and down. Trying not to look guilty. Thinking of anything that I could have done that might have caused a fire. Just then, a fireman appeared in the doorway carrying a fire extinguisher.'

'"It's okay, you can all go back inside now," he said, opening the door.'

'I ran up those stairs like my life depended on it. When I got to the top floor, the door of the flat was wide open. I ran in and quickly surveyed the damage. It wasn't too bad. It wasn't anything like what I'd imagined. The curtain in the lounge was a bit burnt and the ceiling was slightly stained, but everything else seemed okay.'

'"The fireman put it out using a carbon dioxide fire extinguisher," said Connor, appearing in the doorway. "Your tenant came over early this morning to feed his cat and clear out its litter tray. He must have lit a scented candle and forgot to blow it out before he left. The cat must have knocked it off the windowsill, and the curtain caught fire. You're lucky we managed to contain it."'

'The next day, Connor insisted everyone working in the building had to have £5 million-worth of public liability insurance, so I had to down tools and stop working while I sorted it out. Then he refused to accept any deliveries to the front of the building. Then he wouldn't allow Big Pete in because he disapproved of tradesmen with tattoos. So I asked Chris to help me put a new floor down in the bathroom. He drove me mad. He wouldn't stop talking to me about the trestle tables he'd just bought and the benefits of using a bandsaw. By the end of the day, I honestly wished I was deaf. I spent most of the afternoon with tiny pieces of toilet paper shoved into my ears. It was the only way I could stay sane. That evening, when I got home, the tenant called me.'

'"Have you seen my cat?" he said, anxiously.'

'"He's probably in the cupboard in the hall. He likes it in there, he curls up behind the hot-water tank," I said. The cat had been sniffing around us for most of the afternoon. I kept putting it in the lounge but after a few minutes it would reappear. There were some mouse droppings under the floor between the joists, so I presumed it could smell something. Chris was cutting the new floor downstairs, to avoid creating any dust in the flat, while I reconfigured the pipes under the floor. Then we both carried the ply upstairs, slid it into the bathroom and screwed it down. We did it in two pieces so there weren't too many joins. This meant they were big pieces of wood and it was hard to see where we were going when we were carrying them.'

'"It sounds like he's under the floor," said the tenant.'

'I drove straight round. I quickly unscrewed the ply and the cat shot out like its tail was on fire.'

'Just imagine how you would feel if someone did that to Pushkin,' said my daughter.

'I didn't do it deliberately. He must have snuck under there when we were carrying it in,' I replied.

'I can't believe you buried his cat!' she said, looking appalled.

'That's exactly what he said. "I don't want you working here any more!" he screamed.'

'I can understand why he was so upset.'

'So could I, but I honestly didn't do it deliberately. Don't you think he was overreacting?'

'What's all this got to do with dying broke?'

'Ah, I'm getting to that. The next day, all hell broke loose. Layla turned up looking like she'd seen a ghost.'

'Maybe she had?'

'I don't think so. I never saw Noel Coward again. I wish I had. He's my hero.'

'"We've got a problem," Layla told me. "My dad just died."'

'"Oh, I'm so sorry," I told her.'

'"It's a nightmare! It happened yesterday."'

'"Had he been ill?"'

'"No. He had a heart attack. The problem is he gave me the money to buy this flat. Now, I'm going to have to pay inheritance tax on it. My sister wants to keep his house in

Hampstead, so it means we're going to have to sell most of his other properties to pay the taxman. The tax on this place is going to be huge. I don't have that kind of money. Everything I have is tied up in my house."'

'"Can't you borrow it?"'

'"The banks won't lend us any more money. I earn fuck all and my husband trades cryptocurrency. He won't sell it because he's convinced he's going to be the next Bitcoin billionaire. So, it looks like we're just going to have to sell it."'

'"Do you want me to finish the bathroom?"'

'"No. Just leave it. There's no point spending any more money on it. The estate agents think whoever buys it will want to renovate the whole flat. That's what I was going to do. Just tidy it up. It's better to sell it as a blank canvas."'

'Oh no, what happened then?' asked my daughter.

'She sold the flat, paid the tax and I put the bath into our flat. Mum was over the moon,' I said, as we walked back into reception and handed in our headsets. 'What shall we do now?' I said, opening the door. I was nervous. It felt safe in the War Rooms. We were in a routine. What on earth were we going to talk about outside? We climbed the steps and looked out across St James's Park. It had stopped raining and the air was crisp.

'How about lunch? Come on, let's have some fun. I need to start building up some credits, otherwise you'll put me in a crap care home with an aggressive porter who won't let anyone in,' I said, as we walked into the park. Halfway through the park, she took my arm. I almost burst into tears. We walked arm in arm, trying to sidestep the goose shit that was plastered across the pavement.

'I never knew Churchill sent aid to Stalin,' she said, as we crossed the bridge in the centre of the park.

'I guess sometimes you have to give to someone you don't know you can completely trust in order to win the war,' I replied, as we marched towards The Mall.

'Where are we going?' she said, as we walked out of the park.

'It's a surprise,' I replied, as we crossed the road and headed towards Piccadilly. We meandered through the streets, stopping to look in the art-gallery windows and eventually arrived at a restaurant called Richoux. I had been there before and I thought she would like it. It was classy, without being too stuffy. It felt like an elegant French café with its dark-red interior, pristine pastries and slightly subdued lighting. We hadn't really spoken since we left the park. I presumed she'd had enough of the story, but as soon as we sat down she said, 'So what happened to Layla?'

'She kept her father's house in Hampstead, but she had to sell the flat and the rest of his property portfolio. She told me his estate was worth over £3 million pounds and the taxman was going to take a third of it.'

'They lost a million pounds!'

'Yes, it's an interesting life lesson, don't you think?'

'Dad, why are you telling me all this?'

'Look, I know things haven't been brilliant between us and I realised today that I'm probably partly to blame. I didn't know how to handle what you were going through, so I withdrew. I was wrong to do that. I should have tried harder. I should have listened to you. Now, what would you like? I feel like celebrating,' I said, changing the subject as the waiter came over and handed me my napkin. 'Ladies first,' I said, remembering my manners. She quietly told the waiter what she wanted, and I sat back and admired her. I knew then that we were going to be okay. I didn't need to say anything else.

'Dad, is that why our bathroom is so old-fashioned?' she said, smiling.

'How dare you! Our bath might have once belonged to the man who wrote *Blithe Spirit*! It's like bathing with God!'

'How do you know?' she said, laughing.

'I saw him! Remember?' I said, pouring her a glass of fizzy water. We sat there for almost an hour and she told me all about her teenage angst. How she wanted a boyfriend, but didn't know how to get one. How her confidence was underpinned by how she looked. How Jo always tried to reassure her, but she wished she wouldn't because it felt hollow. She completely opened up to me. I sat there and hardly said a word; I just listened. As we were finishing our meal, a very elegantly dressed middle-aged woman, who was sitting at the next table, stood up and turned to her, 'You are a very brave, and very beautiful, young woman,' she said. Then, she looked at me, shook her head, and left.

'Why did she say that?' said my daughter, suddenly looking very self-conscious.

'Probably because she's been sitting there thinking how utterly useless I am. She's probably talking to her friends right now. "You wouldn't believe it. There was this beautiful young woman having lunch next to me, she was opening up to this awful middle-aged man. He looked like some kind of tradesman! She was telling him how she felt and he didn't reassure her once. It was just appalling!"' I said, in the poshest female voice I could muster. 'Sometimes you can't win,' I said returning to my normal voice. 'Now what shall we do next?'

'Can we go shopping?'

'Absolutely. Lead the way,' I said, as I paid the bill.

I often think about that cold, wet winter's day, when we went to the War Rooms together. I've always wondered why I told her that particular plumbing story. Maybe the difficult doorman was symbolic of the impenetrable wall I knew I had to overcome with her. Maybe the over-anxious tenant, whose issues I had to accommodate, was, in fact, her. The bathroom – beautiful, but broken and falling apart – was our relationship. Layla was Jo, trying to get me to fix things between us, and perhaps the bath was symbolic of something that I was hoping to salvage from that day. I don't know, and it doesn't really matter. It broke the ice. It was the first time that one of my plumbing stories had ever really resonated with her. But, as I was telling it, I also realised that I was part of the problem. I needed to stop and listen to her. I was used to recounting my version of events. In my enthusiasm to tell a story, I could be stifling and overbearing.

She needed to tell her stories too, and maybe I was affecting her voice. I was subconsciously stopping her from being heard. It occurred to me that if I ever made a lot of money, I could easily end up doing what Layla's father had done. I realised I needed to start trusting her, so that when it's my turn to hand over the baton, I can do it with confidence, before it's too late. After all, they say you should be kind to your kids because they will choose your care home! She took my arm as we walked out of the restaurant. The sun was peeping through the clouds and people kept pushing past us as we walked down towards Piccadilly Circus, but I didn't care. I felt free, like a huge weight had been lifted. Our war was finally over; now, it was time to rebuild, I thought, as we crossed the road arm in arm and headed towards Regent Street.

13

Facts Are Stranger than Fiction

Several years ago, I injured my right hand and all my fingers except my forefinger turned inwards, creating a kind of claw. This meant I was forced to stop work. So, I went to see a physio to see if he could unfurl my fingers.

'Come in,' he said abruptly, as I apprehensively opened the door. He was a tall, thin man with large glasses, which he wore on the bridge of his nose. 'What seems to be the problem?' he said, encouraging me to sit down on the chair next to his desk. He looked like a clean-shaven Dr Shipman, which slightly freaked me out and, as I was soon to find out, there were other similarities.

'My hand has turned into a claw,' I said, holding it up to show him. 'I can't move the bottom three fingers. Everyone thinks I'm pointing at them,' I joked.

'I see,' he said, examining me, 'You've trapped a nerve in your shoulder.' His manner was very matter of fact.

'No,' I replied, 'It's not in my shoulder, it's in my hand.'

'No, it's not,' he said, pointing to my shoulder. 'It's in here,' as he suddenly leant forward and forced his three longest fingers into my shoulder joint.

'Jesus Christ!' I screamed, jumping backwards. It felt like he'd just poked me with a cattle prod.

'He can't help you in here,' the physio said, laughing, as he moved towards me, menacingly. Then, he did it again. Only, this time, he held them there. I was completely paralysed. Pinned up against the wall, unable to move, with pain streaming down my arm and across my chest. His whole body weight pressed through the tips of his fingers deep into my shoulder joint. Then he started slowly to draw them down across my chest towards my sternum, keeping the pressure on at all times. It felt like he was cutting me open.

'Fuckin' hell,' I screamed.

'I hope they do, for your sake,' he said, laughing. The bastard was enjoying himself. *He's a fucking sadist. I've come to a physio who looks like Doctor Death and likes inflicting pain,* I thought to myself. I wanted to leave, but I had to do something, and he came highly recommended. Besides, I couldn't work with a claw.

'The whole of your right side is in spasm. Take off your trousers and lie down on the table,' he said, writing some notes on his computer. The next half hour was without doubt the most painful of my life. I screamed every obscenity known to man, as the physio dug his hands into every part of my broken body. When it was over, I felt like I'd been beaten up. And the worst thing was, it had made absolutely no difference to my hand; I still had a claw. But, however painful it was and, believe me, it was pretty bloody painful, the pain was nothing in comparison to what was to come.

Back at home, Jo was waiting with her dreaded spreadsheet. The physio appointment was the last in a long line of excuses I had used to try to get out of doing my accounts. I'd already fixed the garden gate, resealed the shower, changed the kitchen tap, unblocked the basin in the downstairs loo, tidied up the garden, replaced some rotten decking, cleared out my van and taken it to the garage so it could be serviced.

Jo had already paired all my socks and hung up all my clothes, because she knew that's what I would do next. When I got home, she was sitting at the kitchen table waiting for me, her laptop open. My heart sank. I felt like I was being summoned into the dock and Jo was the judge. Over the next three days, she would analyse every bit of my business. She would leave no stone unturned; there would be nowhere to hide. I would shout and scream, we'd argue for hours and our marriage would come close to complete collapse. Then, at the end of this hugely painful process, I would impose severe cutbacks on our lifestyle and Jo would sentence me to another year's hard labour, with no possibility of parole. There was no getting out of it; I had to face it. She had already opened Excel.

'Paperwork isn't something I'm particularly good at,' I said, sitting down opposite her, trying to get my excuses in first.

'That's putting it mildly,' she said. She was sitting in exactly the same place she had sat in last year, and that had been disastrous. We hadn't spoken to each other for a week. 'How did it go at the physio?' she said.

'Unbelievably painful. I screamed the whole time. There was an old lady sitting in the waiting room. She looked totally traumatised.'

'Did you swear?'

'Constantly. It was embarrassing. He's a fucking sadist. The bastard kept laughing at me. But I'd rather that than this,' I said, holding up my pointing hand to my head like it was a loaded gun.

She laughed. 'Come on, there are lots of things *I'd* rather be doing, but we have to do it, so stop making excuses. I promise I'll try not to be too judgemental.'

'Can I have that in writing?' I said, momentarily taken in by a false sense of security.

Before I go any further, I should first explain that Jo and I are opposites. This means that our chemistry is uniquely bipolar. She is super-organised and has a filing system that makes Marie Kondo's look disorganised. I am not. My filing system consists of an old Tesco bag full of receipts, a brown A3 envelope full of invoices and an old Co-op bag full of bank statements. Jo does her company accounts every month, so she knows exactly where she is financially at all times. I do mine annually, and don't have a clue. So, doing my accounts always leads to conflict, because it highlights the contrast in our characters. Jo tries to get me to do it myself, but this never happens. So, out of desperation, she begrudgingly offers to help me. This usually happens in the second week of April. The way it works is simple – I sit at one end of the kitchen table and read out every invoice and receipt; she enters them into an Excel spreadsheet. Jo loves Excel, she finds it fun. I hate it. It makes me want to set my own hair on fire.

Jo was waiting. Her spreadsheet was open, her fingers were hovering over the keys. Sheepishly, I went into the bedroom and retrieved the Tesco bag. I walked in and untied the top. She looked at me, trying not to say anything, but I could see what she was thinking.

'What do you want to do first?' I said, trying not to laugh. The tension was palpable. At any moment the arguing was going to start. She wouldn't be able to stop herself. I could see it boiling up inside her.

'Income,' she said, holding it together.

'Okay, I'll get the other bag,' I said.

She smirked as I disappeared back into the bedroom. Two minutes later I appeared with the Co-op bag and sat down opposite her.

'Okay,' I said, composing myself. I opened the bag and thrust my hand deep into it, grabbing the first invoice. It was twelve pages long and read like a short story. I started reading it out loud. She sat there, waiting for me to finish, the smirk on her face concealing the cold fury that her eyes could not. But after five minutes, she cracked.

'Can you just tell me how much you were bloody paid!' she screamed.

Fortunately, we both found it funny. She knew it was the frustrated writer in me – even my invoices read like short stories. The tension lifted, but we both knew this wouldn't last long. For the next few hours I read out the date, the amount and the type of job on every invoice. We became an ultra-efficient accounting machine. We were completely in sync. Like an ocean liner steaming smoothly across the Atlantic, but we were well aware that an enormous iceberg was heading our way. As I read out the last invoice, the lookout raised the alarm and the liner tried to turn, but the iceberg ripped through the side of our ship. We looked at each other, like a couple of sailors waiting for the other to make the first move towards the lifeboat. Then, I stood up and slowly walked over to the shelf in the kitchen where we kept all our bank statements. Jo's were all filed in order. Monthly. Neat. Easy to access. The year was clearly displayed on the spine. Next to her line of perfect ring binders was my old brown paper envelope. In it were all my bank statements. Credit card bills were mixed in with pieces of paper with measurements and bathroom designs sketched on them, along with character observations scribbled onto old bits of cardboard. None of it made any sense. Nothing was in any order. Some months were missing. Jo watched me walk over and place the envelope on the table. She didn't say a word. I tipped the contents out onto the table and started inspecting the mayhem. Then I said it. She'd been waiting for it. She knew it was coming.

'Obviously I don't raise invoices for every job I do,' I said. My words were nonchalant, like it wasn't a big deal. But we both knew it meant we were going to spend the next six hours trying to make sense of something that made no sense. Jo didn't respond, she just sat there quietly while I anxiously tried to put the papers strewn all over the table into some kind of order. But it was just too difficult. Too many months, too many pieces of paper.

'For fuck's sake! This is a bloody joke! It's worse than last year!' she said, leaping to her feet. 'Why didn't you file them when they arrived?'

And that was it. She'd fired the first shot. Now we were at war. For the next three days we would be locked in constant combat; it would be a fight to the death. There would be some moments of calm, brief ceasefires, but they wouldn't last long.

An hour later, we were ready to carry on. *Nothing is going to distract me. I'm a lean, mean accounting machine!* I thought, as I sat down to face her.

'Tell me the name of the person who paid you, the date and how much you were paid,' she said reopening her laptop. It was simple, clear, there was no margin for error. I fiddled nervously with April's bank statement. *I can do this. It doesn't have to end in divorce. This year it's going to be different,* I thought, as she sat patiently at the end of the table.

'Starting when?' I enquired.

'The 6th of April,' she said.

'Okay. Are you ready?'

'Yes, I'm ready,' she said, knowing she'd just got into a car that was destined to crash.

'Lewis, £70, 6th of April.' And I'm off. The starter's pistol has been fired. I'm up and out of the blocks, running at full pelt. Nothing can stop me now. 'Jones, £85, 7th of April. Rogers, £25, 7th of April. Staines, £125, 8th of April. Goldstein, …' I'm in full flow, magnificent, Ben Johnson on steroids.

'Slow down. Is that Laura? What did you do for her?'

'No idea, £50, 7th of April,' I reply. I'm unstoppable. The ship has left Southampton for the second time. 'Silverman, …'

'Oh, is that Valerie?'

'Yes,' I reply, as if to say, 'Don't interrupt me.'

'What did you do for her?' she said, trying get me to slow down.

'Fuck knows! £200, 8th of April. Maybe I changed her shower cartridge, I can't really remember. Patel, £175, 9th of April. Sanchez, £55, 10th of April. Lombardi, £125, 10th of April. Christodoulos, £35, 15th of April. There's a gap. The 10th to 15th of April. We both know why. That was when we did my accounts last year and it ended badly, *really* badly. The wounds have only just healed. So, I carried on, pretending I hadn't clocked it, but we both had. So, I sped up, trying to get away. *If I can just make it to May,* I thought to myself, *I should be far enough away for her not to remember.* 'Roberts, £50, 16th of April. Campbell, £1,750, 25th of April.'

'We've already got that, it was one of your invoices.'

'Okay, scrap that. Moreau, £125, 29th of April. Sembhi, £75, 30th of April.' This went on for hours. When it was time to pick up our daughter from her after-school class, we agreed to stop and carry on the next day. We were both exhausted.

'You've done really well,' she said, adding it all up. 'You made more than last year.'

'Great. Then why haven't we got any money?'

'I don't know,' she said, pretending she didn't know the answer. But she did. We'd deal with that tomorrow. For now, day one was over. We were both still standing and darkness was about to descend. I made a point of putting all my bank statements and credit card bills neatly into a ring binder and promised that I'd do this every time a new one arrived (even though she knew I never would). Then I made her dinner to thank her. We were civil, but, beneath the surface, we both knew we still had a long way to go.

The next morning, I woke early. I brought Jo breakfast in bed, fed the dog, did the washing up and in all other ways behaved as attentively as possible. She knew I was nervous. Doing the income was the easy bit. But today we had to do the expenditure. That was so much worse. It was a minefield, littered with lots of unexploded bombs and, thanks to my unique filing system (or rather my lack of *any* filing system), we were going to have to pick our way through it blindfolded.

'Come on, let's do your outgoings,' she said, almost jovially – *It must be a trick, she knows what's coming,* I thought. She was sitting there waiting for me with a look of apprehension on her face. I sat down and tried to compose myself. The Tesco bag was sitting on the table. There were almost a thousand receipts in it. I knew they weren't in any order. Every receipt for everything I had bought in the last year was in there. I knew they weren't just work receipts. Every year, Jo told me not to put them in, but for some reason I always did.

'I wasn't sure exactly what I could claim,' I said, 'So there might be a few that aren't work-related.' My words hung in the air between us. Neither of us said anything. She knew I was too lazy to sort them out. It didn't matter that we argued about this every year, or that it made it so much more difficult.

I could see Jo's stress levels building. I started riffling through the Tesco bag, trying to find a receipt with an April date. But there were too many. I had only two working fingers, so the receipts kept slipping from my hand.

'For fuck's sake!' she screamed, standing up and tipping the contents of the Tesco bag out onto the table. Anxiously, I started to pick up receipts that had fallen onto the floor.

'Jesus Christ,' she screamed, 'This is even worse than the other bag! What the hell is *this*! *Oddbins*! What the hell is a receipt from Oddbins doing in here?' Her voice was getting higher. The floodgates had opened and soon there would be no way to stop the tidal wave of abuse that was about to be released. Just one more. Just one more receipt would do it. And there it was, sitting on the top of the pile. I tried to grab it, but she got there first. I lifted my hands to cover my head as she read it out loud: 'Lurpak! *Lurpak!*' she screamed, as if saying it twice would make it disappear. 'A bunch of bananas and a fucking baguette!'

She was apoplectic as she started whacking me over the head with the Tesco bag. 'A fucking baguette,' she kept screaming. I couldn't stop laughing, but the more I laughed, the angrier she got. I curled up on the floor, unable to contain myself, tears of laughter rolling down my face. Then, suddenly, she stopped. 'I can't do this any more,' she said. This was a very bad sign. It meant she'd already reached saturation point and we hadn't even started yet. Soon, her anger would turn to hatred. I did my best to placate her, but it was too late. The day was over. We would have to regroup in the morning.

The next day, we started again. Jo was calm, unemotional, businesslike. I read out each receipt and she entered it into her spreadsheet, just as we had been doing two days before. Only this time it was much more painful. There weren't any interruptions, apart from occasionally arguing about whether something was tax-deductible or not. Jo was looking at me like she wanted to kill me; I was looking at her as if I wanted her to.

After about an hour, I felt like I was going cross-eyed. Reading receipts was having a bizarre effect on my brain: supplier, date, amount; supplier, date, amount.

I wanted to die. Anything would be better than this. I started praying for my phone to ring, but it didn't.

My mind began to wander. I noticed Jo was wearing a very tight top. I was watching her typing, inputting my expenses into her super-sexy spreadsheet. I wanted to take her there and then, but I couldn't – she was too busy. So, I started flirting with her. Supplier, date, amount. It was unbearable. Her fingers gliding quickly over the keys. I noticed her French manicure, her perfume. *It had been ages since we'd had sex in the kitchen. Who was I kidding? We'd never had sex in the kitchen! Perhaps now could be the time?* She knew what I was thinking. She smiled at me, flattered. Her eyes closed slightly, coyly. I moved towards her, reading out a receipt: supplier, date, amount.

'Don't even think about it,' she said quietly.

It felt like she'd thrown a bucket of freezing cold water over my bollocks. Supplier, date, amount. Supplier, date, amount. I started trying to think of ways to escape. Under the table I texted my brother the beer emoji, code to call me with an emergency. Two minutes later, my phone rang. I answered it and put it on speaker, so Jo could hear.

'We've got water pissing out from behind our dishwasher,' he said. Then I heard him turn on his kitchen tap to add to the dramatic effect.

'Christ, it sounds terrible! Don't worry, I'm on my way,' I said, looking at Jo apologetically. My brother lives in Kent; it would take me hours to get there. But she knew what I was up to. She knew I wasn't going to drive to Kent, I was going to the pub. But she didn't say anything. It was easier to get on with it herself. I was just a distraction.

When I got home that night, it was pitch black outside. Jo had taken the light bulb out of the outside light, so I couldn't see what I was doing. She'd quadruple-locked the front door to make it almost impossible for me to get in. She knew I was going to be pissed. It was like *The Krypton Factor* for people who were worse for wear. I struggled to get the key in the lock. Jo was awake, but pretending not to be. She was furious. She had spoken to my sister-in-law and found out that the flood behind their dishwasher was a load of bollocks. She had locked the bedroom door and wouldn't let me in, so I was forced to sleep on the couch.

The next day I woke up with the dog's arse in my face. I felt terrible. My clothes stank, the room smelled of farts and I felt like I'd inhaled an ashtray. My eyes were bloodshot and my brain was banging against the inside of my skull. Jo was doing everything she could to torture me. She knew I had a terrible hangover, so she kept using the blender. Then she called the physio and paid for me to have another three sessions. I apologised for my bad behaviour, but it wasn't enough. She ignored me and started hoovering, banging the vacuum cleaner into every piece of furniture and every skirting board. So I left and went out for breakfast. When I got back, she was sitting at the kitchen table, entering the last of my receipts into her spreadsheet, slamming each one down ever more aggressively onto the table. She may have been angry, but she also wanted to show me what she had done; she was craving some recognition for all her hard work. So I stood behind her as she scrolled down her epically long spreadsheet. It was absolutely amazing. I wanted to hug and kiss her, but it was far too soon for that. It would be weeks before that could happen. Without speaking, she simply showed me all the expenses she wasn't sure I could claim. It was a trap; she was begging me to say something, daring me to. Whatever I said it would be wrong. Then, she would bite my head off and storm out. Slowly, she scrolled down, pointing out things she knew I thought should be included. I could see her game, so I kept quiet. Until she reached Specsavers.

'What's that?' I said. I knew I'd made a mistake as soon as I said it, but it was too late.

'It's your glasses,' she said, her eyes widening slightly, waiting for me to respond.

'I'm sure I can claim for them,' I said. But my nerves had got the better of me and I had said it far too aggressively, so that it sounded like an accusation. I didn't mean it; it just came out that way. 'I can't work if I can't see what I'm doing,' I said, trying to salvage the situation, but it was too late.

'You can do the rest yourself, you bastard,' she said, closing her computer and storming off. She was right: I *was* a bastard. Doing my accounts brought out the worst in me – I couldn't help it. I behaved like a bolshie teenager. Fortunately, she'd completed the job. The next day, she sent it to The Royal Ballet School, so they could work out how much they were going to charge for Oli's education. And that was it; it was all over.

I had my usual panic about not living within our means and did an immediate stock check of all our outgoings. Anything that wasn't essential was immediately cut: Netflix and Amazon Prime were the first to go, but that wasn't enough. Drastic cutbacks were required. And that was it, Austerity April had begun. I stopped drinking, turned the heating off, became a pescatarian, skipped lunch and did every job I could, even if it was outside London. It was brutal. Breakfast was banned. I stopped driving unless it was absolutely necessary (to save on petrol). Jo went along with it, but she knew it wouldn't last. She pretended to cancel things, but didn't. Once I was satisfied that all the cutbacks were complete, I went back to work. I lived like a monk, but after a month of working all hours on a diet of canned tuna and rice cakes, I cracked and overruled all my new rules, because, let's face it, life is too short, and we could all be run over by a bus tomorrow. And that was the end of it, our whole sorry saga limped on for another year. But there were two final obstacles right at the end of the track, which had to be overcome. Every year, they drove me to distraction, but there was nothing I could do to avoid them.

The next day I pulled up outside my plumbing merchant. John, my favourite shop assistant, was sitting behind his desk, looking slightly shifty. 'Watch out, here comes the claw,' he said as soon as I walked into the shop. 'What are you after?'

'A new shower valve,' I said, inspecting the selection on the wall next to his desk.

'Which one? Can you point to it,' he said, smiling.

'Very funny,' I said, pulling my right hand out of my pocket. My bottom three fingers were still curled up into the palm of my hand.

'How can you work with that?' he said, laughing.

'With great difficulty. I just point and have to get other people to do it.'

'Oh, by the way, I've got something for you,' he said, rummaging around on his desk. I wanted to turn and run, but it was too late; he had it in his hand.

'That better not be what I think it is.'

'It must have got lost,' he said, trying to get his excuse in first.

'I told you, I've finished my accounts. That's why I came in and settled up with you last week. If it's for anything before the 6th of April, you can forget it.'

'How much is it?' I said, snatching it out of his hand.

'Two-and-a-half grand!'

'For fuck's sake John, Jo's going to kill me.'

When I got home that evening, I showed Jo the invoice.

'I had to pay it,' I said.

'Why?'

'Let's just say if I didn't, I'd be treading water in the Thames right now.'

'Sounds good to me,' she said, smiling. She still hadn't forgiven me. I'd only just been readmitted to the bedroom, but a Berlin Wall of pillows had been built down the middle of the bed, so I couldn't get anywhere near her.

'You'll have to claim it next year', she said, handing me a new Tesco bag.

'I don't know what I would do without you,' I said, leaning forward to kiss her on the forehead.

'You'd probably be in prison for failing to do your tax return. Come to think of it, that's not such a bad idea! At least then I wouldn't have to do your bloody accounts every year,' she said, with a broad grin.

The final obstacle was a lot more complicated. Doing my accounts had a bizarre effect on my mental health. For months, I would keep waking up in the middle of the night, worrying about all the jobs I'd forgotten I'd done until I did my accounts. They acted like a kind of catalyst: all my plumbing nightmares came flooding back to me and started running on a loop inside my head. So, I would get up and pace around the flat. I knew it was just my overactive imagination torturing me, but that didn't stop me replaying all the catastrophes I'd avoided and close shaves that I'd had, and imagining what might have happened. I called them my 'pipe dreams'. I had a reservoir of them in my brain. As I paced round the flat, I started moulding them into stories that I could tell. Then, when I was happy with them, I told them to Jo. She loved them and encouraged me to tell all our friends. Humour has always been the way to her heart. I regurgitated them at dinner parties and she finally forgave me for all my appalling behaviour.

'You should write them down,' she said, congratulating me after one of my recitals. I knew she was right, but I never had the time. No matter how hard I worked, we never had enough money for me to stop plumbing. I couldn't write and plumb at the same time. I'd tried, but I found it impossible. I ended up being bad at both. And being a bad plumber was a lot worse than being a bad writer. Then, the pipe dreams would be off the scale! But, bizarrely, this was all about to change and those plumbing nightmares, which had tormented me for years, were about to become my biggest asset.

I didn't know it, but in less than a year, the whole world was about to be turned upside down. Governments around the globe would impose nationwide lockdowns. I'd be forced to stop working and all those years of accounts that Jo had done would finally pay us a dividend, because I would be compensated for not being able to work. The next time we sat down to do my accounts, I couldn't desert her and go to the pub – because they were all closed. We had to work through my accounts as a team and make all the necessary cutbacks together, because we didn't know how long the pandemic was going to last. Austerity April ended up lasting the rest of the year and, at the end of it, we had finally figured out how to live within our means. In many ways, it brought us closer together. I did all the DIY jobs that Jo had been nagging me about for years. Then, she didn't sentence me to another year's hard labour; instead, she encouraged me to sit down and write. And when I did, it was like I'd turned on the tap. The stories just came pouring out of me. Who'd have thought that those pipe dreams would become the basis of a book, that a global pandemic would give me the time to finally write it and, having spent a whole year in excruciating pain at the hands of a sadistic physio to get my right hand back, I wouldn't actually need it, because I type using just my two forefingers? Sometimes, facts really are a lot stranger than fiction!

Acknowledgements

I'd like to thank my agent, Robert Smith, for championing me and my editor, Duncan Proudfoot, for believing in the book's potential. I'd also like to thank Hazel and Genio for their constant support (and in Hazel's case for also being such a good sport; I love her to bits); Sally, Toby and Amelie for encouraging me to write it; Dame Jo for reading every chapter and being so diplomatic with her feedback; and Ziggi, Emily, Andrew and Spiney for giving me such honest and helpful suggestions.